HOW DO YOU FEEL ABOUT DRINKING?

Here's what some teenagers say about drinking in

BOMBED, BUZZED, SMASHED, OR . . . SOBER:

KATHY: I don't drink to get drunk. I drink because I like the taste and because it makes me feel good. . . . When you drink, all you think about is the good, all the nice things in life. You're relaxed.

LINDA: Alcohol, yuk! Getting drunk must be the worst feeling. No, I guess it isn't really, but it's pretty bad.

BETH: I think really drunk people are funny or obnoxious. I hate alcoholics and have no pity for anyone who gets that way. If I'm going to get fried, I mean really zonked, I like to do that with other people who will be just as bad off. That way, I don't get embarrassed, I don't stand out.

MEL: I drink to make me feel good. Sometimes I'm kind of mixed up and drinking seems to soothe my head. I get nervous easy and it helps me out. Other people are an influence also. If everyone is drinking, it's kind of hard not to, and anyway, I really don't see anything wrong with it. If you want to, why not?

BOMBED, BUZZED, SMASHED, OR... SOBER

John Langone

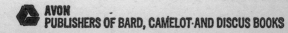

AVON
PUBLISHERS OF BARD, CAMELOT·AND DISCUS BOOKS

AVON BOOKS
A division of
The Hearst Corporation
959 Eighth Avenue
New York, New York 10019

Copyright © 1976 by John Langone
Published by arrangement with Little, Brown & Company.
Library of Congress Catalog Card Number: 76-8490
ISBN: 0-380-43653-1

First Avon Printing, April, 1979
Second Printing

AVON TRADEMARK REG. U.S. PAT. OFF. AND IN
OTHER COUNTRIES, MARCA REGISTRADA,
HECHO EN U.S.A.

Printed in the U.S.A.

*To my good friend John A. Hahn,
who taught me much about journalism,
this book is affectionately dedicated.*

Acknowledgments

———◆◆◆———

Sources consulted in the preparation of this book have been cited whenever possible. I am particularly indebted to the National Institute of Alcohol Abuse and Alcoholism, to the American Medical Association and to the Francis A. Countway Library of Medicine at the Harvard Medical School. My special thanks to Ms. Donna Thomas, English teacher at Central Junior High School, Hingham, Massachusetts, and Mr. John Hennelly, English teacher at Hingham High School. I would like to state that while the quotations used at the beginning of each chapter are based on interviews, the name assigned to each quotation is fictional. While I am grateful to all who have helped, I alone am responsible for the book's point of view and any errors it contains.

John Langone
Hingham, Massachusetts
November, 1975

Contents

What Do You Know
about Drinking?

———◆◆◆———

KATHY: I drink because after going to school all week I look forward to Friday and Saturday nights, to relax, to have an enjoyable time and party. I enjoy the taste. Lots of people like the after-effects. I don't drink to get drunk, I drink because I like the taste and because it makes me feel good. When you're listening to the stereo, you can get in the mood for it better if you drink. You forget about the bad things that happened or that are going to happen. When you drink, all you think about is the good, all the nice things in life. You're relaxed.

JACK: I drink beer a lot. But if I have the money I drink hard stuff. I try to get totally blitzed every time. I don't get sick too often, like once every six months. I also think it's funny when chicks get blitzed, they're all over the place. Only thing I hate is the hiccups that I get sometimes, it bugs the hell out of me. But I really do like getting blasted.

———◆◆◆———

Most of you have taken a drink now and then, and by that I mean, of course, that you've tried alcoholic beverages—beer, wine and liquor. And you've done it with or without the consent of your parents. Just like a lot of you have tried pot and pills. For some of you, it was just something to do once or twice, and then forget and not bother with again. Some of you probably drink on occasion, at a party or at home with your meals. Some of you have been high, even drunk. The rest of you got no reaction, or you got sick, threw up and vowed you'd never drink again. Maybe you've felt guilty when you've hidden the fact of your

11

drinking or your experiments with liquor from your parents, or maybe you've been found out and punished severely. Or, your parents made a joke of the time you came home after having had too much to drink, told you it happens to everyone—and then dropped the subject. A small number of you are hooked, really dependent, really into it; no one knows how many except maybe the package store dealer who sells it, and sometimes he'd rather just keep it quiet.

So you drink. But what do you really know about the drinks you've tried or use now? What do you know about alcohol and its effect on the body and mind? About alcoholism, about its causes? Do you know when a person is considered drunk? How many drinks it takes? Do you know the difference between a problem drinker and an alcoholic? Do you know what a social drinker is? Do you know what the warning signs are that someone is heading into the wrong kind of drinking? What about treatment for someone with a drinking problem? Can he or she be cured? Lastly, do you know the right way to drink? Have you heard the term "responsible drinking"?

This book might be a bit different from others you may have read on the subject. If you have read anything about alcohol, chances are fairly good that much of what it said was that alcohol is wrong, period, so don't get started on it and you won't have any troubles later on. That's good advice—for some people—but it's not as easy as it sounds. Some of you, of course, may never ever drink; and you are to be respected for that decision. There is nothing that says you have to, and it's never impolite to refuse a drink.

But the fact is, a lot of you do drink, and will continue to do so. Because of that, teenage drinking problems are increasing—not because you drink, but because some of you don't know how.

So, it's best that you know as much about drinking as possible, because the more you know, the better you'll be able to handle it, either now when you're just starting in to sample it, or later on, if it becomes a part of your life-style.

In two previous books for readers of your age group, I tried to dispel some of the hang-ups we all have about death and dying, and the myths and misconceptions about mental illness and mental retardation, by presenting as many facts, by giving as much information as possible.

I felt strongly, and still feel, that the time to tell you about taboo subjects like those is before you're out of junior or senior high school. I feel the same about this book. There are still adults who consider alcohol a taboo subject for young people. They either haven't realized that teenagers drink, or they have the idea that you should learn about alcohol and drinking when you reach drinking age.

I hope this book will help you to understand what drinking is all about. I hope you'll find out something you didn't know before but have always been curious about. I hope also it will help you decide whether to drink or not if you haven't made a choice yet.

But before we go on, let's see what you do and don't know about liquor and drinking. The answers to the following true or false quiz will be found in various parts of the book. Some of them will probably surprise you and, I have a feeling, some of your parents.

1. Alcohol is a food.
2. Alcohol is a drug.
3. Alcohol is a stimulant.
4. A martini is stronger than a shot of whiskey.
5. Liquor of 100 proof contains 50 percent alcohol.
6. A four-ounce glass of wine, a twelve-ounce can of beer and an ounce of vodka contain about the same amount of alcohol.
7. Drinking coffee is the best way to sober up.
8. Intoxication and alcoholism are the same thing.
9. Liquor in any quantity has a bad effect on the body.
10. Everyone reacts the same way to the same amount of alcohol.
11. Liquor will go to your head faster if you've eaten.
12. There is one cause of alcoholism and that is alcohol.
13. Alcohol contains calories.
14. It is better to sip a drink slowly.
15. Drinking alone is a danger signal.
16. Liquor can kill because it is a poison.
17. Most heavy drinkers are alcoholics.
18. All alcoholics are heavy drinkers.
19. Alcoholism can be cured.
20. Alcohol can make you depressed.
21. Liquor mixed with water will affect you faster than liquor drunk straight.

22. It's best not to drive a car right after even one drink.

23. Psychotherapy is the only way to treat someone with a drinking problem.

24. There is one-half ounce of pure alcohol in a twelve-ounce can of beer.

25. A person's emotional state can affect his or her reaction to alcohol.

26. Alcoholism is an illness.

27. Alcoholism is a crime.

28. Heroin and alcohol can cause physical dependence.

29. You have to drink at least a pint of liquor a day to become an alcoholic.

30. Skid row produces the majority of alcoholics.

31. You can get drunker by switching drinks.

32. Most alcoholics are men.

33. If a person sips a drink slowly over an hour he or she will probably not feel any effects.

34. You can't become an alcoholic by drinking only wine.

35. Beer and wine have a slower effect than liquor.

36. Alcohol goes directly to the brain.

37. You can sober up by dousing your head in cold water or taking a cold shower.

38. Moderate drinkers seem to live longer than people who abstain.

39. It is not yet known whether alcoholism can be inherited.

40. Heavy drinkers know less about alcohol than do abstainers or light drinkers.

41. Ethnic background, socioeconomic status, education and occupation affect the way we drink.

One

A Brief History of Drinking

———◆◆◆———

ELENA: I see kids totaled a lot at my school. It's a blast to drink with other kids, though. Adults don't like the idea of kids drinking, but I don't see what's wrong with it. If kids want to drink, they should. We've been restricted so much that we should be allowed to drink and have fun. We have parties and they get closed down. Oh well, they don't want us drinking I guess. And we're almost eighteen.

———◆◆◆———

Somewhere back in the dawn of history, Satan (or God, according to another version of the legend) came to Noah and offered to assist him in planting grapevines. The man who was destined to become history's most celebrated shipwright accepted—and, coincidentally, some of the animals who had played a major role in Noah's earlier sail to the top of Mount Ararat became associated with alcohol. In turn, a lamb, a lion, a monkey and a pig were slain, and their blood sprinkled over the new vines, and a legacy was left for future generations of drinkers. It was said that we mimic each of the four slain animals according to the amount of liquor consumed: remaining somewhat innocent and meek as the lamb after a little liquor, gaining the courage and bluster of the lion after more, playing the clowning monkey with still more, and finally, becoming bloated as grossly as the pig who does not know his capacity.

From Noah's grapevines to the glistening vats of modern breweries and distilleries may seem like a giant leap across time, but the truth is that while manufacturing methods have become more sophisticated, the basic process of fermentation by which sugar is converted to alcohol remains the same—as have the reasons why people consume alcoholic beverages.

Humankind discovered early that alcohol has value as well as potential for misuse. It has always been a social lubricant to help promote good cheer and lively conversation, a tranquilizer to mask anxiety and calm nerves, an appetite sharpener, a flavoring agent in foods, an aid to digestion, an anesthetic, a preservative, a sacramental agent in religious ceremonies. "I charge thee before God and the Lord Jesus," said Paul to Timothy in Ephesus, "drink no longer only water, but use a little wine for thy stomach's sake." Indeed, the Bible has much to say, a good deal of it favorable, about wine. For example: "Give strong drink unto him that is ready to perish, and wine unto those that be of heavy heart. Let him drink, and forget his poverty, and remember his misery no more." (Proverbs, 31:6, 7) Or, "Let us eat and drink, for tomorrow we shall die." (Isaiah, 22:13). Wine was served, of course, at the Last Supper, and it graced every Roman table. The ancient Greeks, who breakfasted on meat and wine, joined drinking clubs and found such a common bond in membership that their organizations grew into strong political forces. The Romans' Bacchus and the Greeks' Dionysus were the purple-robed, vine-crowned gods of wine, and festivals were held in their honor.

The intoxicating drinks quaffed by the ancients and believed to contain a divine spirit consisted of wines made from grapes and other fruits, and beers made from several kinds of grain. Virtually anything that would undergo fermentation was fodder for these early liquor manufacturers—from palm juice for an Indian drink known as arrack, to mare's milk that resulted in araka in Tartary. The ancient Incas boiled corn, chewed it, and their saliva converted the starch to sugar. Mixed with water, the chewed concoction went into a pot with other ingredients, was boiled and set aside until the conversion to alcohol was achieved. The Aztecs made their brew from cactus sap, the Egyptians from dates.

Beer ranks among the world's oldest intoxicants, with a history recorded in Egyptian hieroglyphics on temple walls and in the chemical traces of barley and yeast cells, from which it is brewed, in five-thousand-year-old urns discovered by archaeologists. During the time of the pharaohs, the honor of brewing beer, as well as baking bread (beer might well have been discovered when bread crumbs dropped into water and fermented) went to the high priests who not only dispensed it but offered it to the gods and even watered their crops with it so that the mysterious power it contained would yield a better harvest. Papyri of the time of Seti I (1300 B.C.) mention a person inebriated from overindulgence in beer.

While the Greeks and Romans viewed beer as a drink for barbarians, they drank it nonetheless, after having acquired the art of brewing from the Egyptians. A beverage made from barley is mentioned by Tacitus in the first century after Christ, and the people of northern Europe consumed enormous quantities of a potent beverage fermented from honey, called mead. Pliny mentions the use of beer in Spain and Gaul: "The natives who inhabit the west of Europe," wrote the Latin author, "have a liquid with which they intoxicate themselves, made from corn and water. The manner of making this liquid is somewhat different in Gaul, Spain and other countries, and is called by different names, but its nature and properties are everywhere the same. The people in Spain, in particular, brew this liquid so well that it will keep good a long time. So exquisite is the cunning of mankind in gratifying their vicious appetites that they have thus invented a method to make water itself produce intoxication." The medieval English monasteries brewed ales that became known for their excellence—not due, apparently, to any divine intervention but to the fact that some of the monasteries held land situated near bodies of water especially good for brewing.

Alcoholic beverages were probably known in the New World long before Columbus, and were certainly brought to America in 1607 with the settling of the Virginia Colony. Beer even made history here, according to Rabbi R. Brasch, who notes in his book *How Did It Begin?* that it was because their casks were almost empty that the Pilgrim fathers aboard the *Mayflower* decided to shorten their voyage and look for a port ahead of schedule: "For we could not take time for further search and consideration, our victuals being much spent, especially beer."

The early New England colonists were heavy drinkers. They imbibed beer at first from America's first brewery built in 1637 by Captain Sedgwick of the Bay Colony, then later used the stronger distilled spirits—brandy, rum and whiskey—which came into general use in the 1600s.

Formerly called *aqua vitae*, or water of life, distilled liquors are beverages of higher alcoholic content than beer or wine, and may be made from wine, as is brandy; from cider, as applejack; or from fermented mixtures to produce rum from molasses or whiskey from grain mash. The first record of distillation was that of an Arabian physician, Abul Kasim, in the tenth century; the pirates, of course, had their yo-ho-ho's and bottles of rum, the manufacture of which prompted this observation by an English visitor to the Caribbean Island of Barbados in 1651: "The chief fudling they make in the Island is Rumbullion, alias Kill Devill, and this is made of sugar canes distilled, a hott, hellish and terrible liquor."

Despite the evils of Demon Rum, it became a major item of trade between the colonies and the West Indies, and brewing beer ranked next in importance to milling and baking. J. C. Furnas has this interesting account of the colonists' drinking habits in his book *The Americans*:

A typical man of the period started the day with a pre-breakfast dram of straight rum, whiskey or peach brandy, depending on his colony. The abstemious, like President-to-be John Adams, confined themselves to a mug or two of hard cider to get the blood stirring. With every meal, practically all . . . drank beer, cider or spirits and water mixed rather stiff to be sure of counteracting the ill effects of water. An eight-year-old girl from Barbados at school in Boston in 1719 wrote to her father complaining that her grandmother, who was boarding her, made her drink water, and father, duly annoyed, insisted that she get beer or wine as befitted her social station. Apprentices and journeymen in forge, mill or shipyard expected grog at the master's expense midmorning and mid-evening. Farm hands harvesting hay or grain laid down the scythe every other round to have another pull at the jug of rum and molasses in the fence corner.

The main point of every apple tree north of the Carolinas, says Furnas, was the hard cider "that was replacing beer down the American gullet." One Yankee village of forty families, he adds, is known to have made three thousand barrels of cider in the year 1721.

Virtually anything can be carried too far, and drinking certainly fits this axiom. Even Noah handled the produce of the first vineyard badly. Drinking his newly-made wine, Noah, the Bible tells us, "was made drunk and was uncovered in his tent." The Scriptures, along with their more positive pronouncements on drink, also have their strong words against it: "The drunkard and the glutton shall come to poverty." (Proverbs 23:21) "Drink not wine nor strong drink, and eat not any unclean thing." (Judges 13:4) "It is good neither to eat flesh, nor to drink wine, nor any other thing whereby thy brother stumbleth." (Romans 14:21) Most of the Bible's warnings, however, deal with drinking to excess, and the Puritans, contrary to popular opinion, did not prohibit the use of beverage alcohol but urged moderation if it had to be consumed. In the Virginia Colony, a law decreed that any person found drunk for the first time was to be reproved privately by the minister; the second time it happened, publicly; the third time, to "lye in halter" for twelve hours and pay a fine. Despite such a law, the same year the Virginia Assembly passed another encouraging the manufacture of wines and distilled spirits in the colony.

Some groups, of course, do preach total abstinence from alcoholic beverages, the Buddhists and Muhammadans among them; and in China in the eleventh century, B.C., one emperor went so far as to order the uprooting of all vines. (A modern day parallel might be the recent decision to stop raising poppies in Turkey in an effort to curb the abuse of heroin which derives from the opium found in the flowered herbs.) But by and large, the message is moderation. "Drunkenness," warned Pythagoras, the Greek philosopher, "brings ruin to everything—self, home and business." Aristotle, too, urged moderation, not only in drinking but in all the enjoyments and activities of life, including eating, working and playing. It was his principle of the Golden Mean which held that virtue occupies a middle ground between extremes.

Moderation and temperance are synonymous, but somehow the latter word took on a narrower meaning in the United States in the 1800s with the organization of the temperance movement, dedicated not to moderation in the use of alcohol but to abstinence. A signer of the

Declaration of Independence, Dr. Benjamin Rush, a physician-general in the Continental Army, was among those who led the attack against liquor, and his pamphlet, *An Inquiry Into the Effects of Ardent Spirits on the Human Body and Mind*, published in 1784, was distributed widely. Five years later, the first temperance society in America was founded in Litchfield, Connecticut, by two hundred farmers who pledged not to give strong liquor to their farm workers. By the time Dr. Rush died in 1831, a number of groups had been organized, among them the Connecticut Society for the Reformation of Morals, aimed at eliminating drunkenness, gambling and lawless behavior, and the Massachusetts Society for the Suppression of Intemperance. The earlier societies often did not object to wine, cider or malt liquors—in fact, a brewery was constructed in Boston to counter the use of distilled liquor—but they spoke out loudly against the immorality of "spirituous beverages." They published and distributed pamphlets and textbooks, held public meetings and national and international conventions. A number of distilleries began to close as the movement gained momentum and membership in the societies swelled. The success of the campaign forced a change in the goal, and beer and wine were included in the ban against drinking. This new hard-line—teetotalism, as it is often called—met some opposition at first from members of the temperance movement who believed strongly that the Bible did not disapprove of the use of wine. But by 1869, the teetotalers had won out, and a number of other groups were springing up, the most powerful of which were the Woman's Christian Temperance Union, founded in 1874, and the Anti-Saloon League, founded in 1893.

Stories like the following from a turn of the century temperance publication were popular:

A little girl was very ill. She was a child of thorough abstainers who allowed no intoxicating drink to enter their house. The doctor had wanted for some time to prescribe stimulants, and, at last, as she grew worse, he insisted, and said that she must take brandy to save her life. "You would not let your child die before your eyes," he said angrily to her father. "You would not surely let your child die for the sake of your foolish fad!"

The father thought it over. Should he bring in the hateful drink, or should he let his child die as the doctor had said, for want of it? Most reluctantly, he went and fetched some brandy, and took it upstairs to his wife, and told her he had consented to give it to the child.

"Have you?" she exclaimed, with horror. "But I have not!" And with a firm hand she put it away into the cupboard.

At the doctor's next visit he found the little child much better.

"So you got the brandy?" he said, turning to the father.

"Yes, sir, I got it," the father replied, looking down to hide a smile.

"Ha, yes," said the doctor, "and you see the effect. It was just the turning-point. If you had not got that brandy your child would have been dead. And now I have every hope of saving her."

The brandy remained in the cupboard and the child got well, but the parents did not venture to tell the doctor what they had done with his prescription.

It was 11 years after this that the mother was taken dangerously ill. A teetotal doctor had set up in the place a short time before, and they sent for him. After examining his patient, he said to her daughter, "I do not often prescribe stimulants but this is a case which requires it. You must get your mother a little brandy."

The daughter remembered her own case. She was but a girl of 19, but she ventured to say to him, "I think you are mistaken, doctor."

"What?" he asked, not believing his ears.

"I cannot give mother brandy," she replied in a trembling voice.

"Indeed! Then I shall speak to your father."

He went upstairs and told the father in peremptory tones, "You must get some brandy for your wife. She needs it absolutely to save her life."

But his former experience had made the father brave. "No, sir," he said sturdily. "If I had wanted a brandy doctor I should not have sent for you, begging your pardon, sir."

And as her daughter had done 11 years before, the mother got well—without the brandy.

Not so peaceful in her rejection of liquor was Carrie Nation, a vocal temperance agitator who, in the early 1900s, became convinced that she was divinely chosen to destroy saloons. Armed with her favorite weapon, a hatchet, she began wrecking barrooms in Medicine Lodge, Kansas, referring to her wave of destruction as "hatchetations." Mrs. Nation was jailed often and generally ridiculed, but she seemed to thrive on the publicity and in 1904 published *The Use and Need of the Life of Carrie A. Nation.*

For some time, the antidrink forces—whose numbers included well-meaning and reasoned citizens as well as eccentrics, fanatics and professional crusaders—most often launched their attacks from the pulpit, from a moral base, Bible in hand, a hymn on their lips. The National Prohibition Party had been formed; its aim was to make illegal the preparation, sale and transport of alcoholic beverages. There had been earlier, short-lived attempts to prohibit such sales, particularly to Indians, and before the Civil War a number of states approved prohibition legislation. But, in all but Maine, they were declared unconstitutional or repealed. Between 1880 and 1900, the movement was renewed in the Middle West, and prohibition laws were passed in Iowa, Kansas and the Dakotas. Other states followed suit, and by the time World War I broke out the persistence of the prohibitionists was beginning to pay off. On December 18, 1917, Congress submitted the Eighteenth Amendment to the Constitution to the states for ratification. This amendment, which would make the entire United States "dry," became effective January 16, 1920, enforced by the Volstead Act which Congress had passed earlier over the veto of President Wilson. Bars, package stores and breweries were closed and no one was able to buy a glass of beer, a bottle of wine or a pint of whiskey. At least not legally. For on the heels of Prohibition, the "noble experiment" it was called, came widespread flaunting of the law, and despite the strictness of the Volstead Act, enforcement proved virtually impossible. It is important to note that the public generally did not regard drinking as a crime, and neither did most of the law enforcement officials from those high up in authority to the patrolman on the beat, who enjoyed a drink now and then themselves. For some, the sudden shift from "wet" to "dry" was akin to the water company's shutting off the water, or the government's ordering the burning of all tobacco crops. Even President Warren Harding, in office during Prohibition, kept a well-stocked bar in the White House.

"Home brew," beer made in stone crocks from malt extract purchased at the many stores that sprang up, came into the language. Pressure cookers fitted with copper tubing, "stills," served the taste of those who wanted stronger drink in the form of "moonshine" liquor. Many moonshiners managed to make a comfortable living just selling in their neighborhoods at a dollar a pint. Some of their wares, however, were not of the best quality, and a number of deaths and ill effects were reported among people who consumed crude batches of so-called bathtub gin, or, in desperation, such dangerous concoctions as "rubby-dub," which was shaving lotion or rubbing alcohol mixed with flavoring extracts. Millions of gallons of industrial alcohol, the poisons removed from it, also were diverted and made into liquor by enterprising individuals with a good working knowledge of chemistry and denaturing processes. Medicinal compounds, some containing 20 percent alcohol, were popular until the government cracked down on this camouflage. Yet some legal liquor was still available in bonded warehouses, designed to be dispensed by doctor's prescription, and those who knew the right doctor had little difficulty getting supplied.

Aside from these sources, there was plenty of other liquor available. Much of it was smuggled into the country from the West Indies by rumrunners in high-speed motorboats, or trucked across the border from Canada; most of this contraband was sold in speakeasies—hangouts known to virtually everyone, including the police. No price was too high for "the real stuff, just off the boat."

Inevitably, bootlegging became big business for organized crime, and the names of Al "Scarface" Capone and "Bugs" Moran dominated the sprawling liquor industry that had begun to grow outside the law. Protected both by the machine gun—which, along with the hip flask, became a symbol of the era—and corrupt public officials, racketeers collected over two billion dollars a year in the sale of illegal liquor during the height of Prohibition. (Other estimates put the figure at some $10 million a day.) Boasted one Chicago police chief: "Sixty percent of my men are bootlegging." Violence flared often and death came sud-

23

denly to hundreds—in gang wars, in gun battles with federal agents and in the murders of hijackers who stole liquor trucks from bootleggers.

By the mid 1920s, opposition to Prohibition began to mount. Spearheaded by such organizations as the Association Against the Prohibition Amendment and the Woman's Organization for the Repeal of National Prohibition, the evils that Prohibition had spawned began to dawn on the public. There was the case of a Michigan widow, imprisoned for life for making home brew because she had been convicted of the charge four times and, under the state law, the life sentence was mandatory for the "crime." An incident off Rhode Island also added to the public clamor against the antiliquor laws. In the early morning of December 28, 1929, a coast guard cutter patrolling through the fog suddenly played its searchlight on a forty-foot boat that was no stranger to the area's waters. It was the *Black Duck*, a sleek rumrunner chased often by the coast guard. The boat turned sharply and tried to dodge the torrent of bullets that burst from the cutter's machine gun. But this time she was unsuccessful. Boarding the *Black Duck*, the coast guardsmen found the bodies of three men; a fourth was badly wounded. They also found several hundred bottles of liquor, apparently to be used at New Year's Eve parties. However, stung by the slayings, the Reverend Roy W. Magoun said indignantly in a sermon the next day in Saint George's Church in Newport: "The deaths of these men must bring to us a little more clearly the horrible price we are paying in attempting to enforce laws which are fundamentally un-American and un-Christian."

The "noble experiment" ended with the vote of Utah on December 5, 1933, as the thirty-sixth state to ratify the Twenty-first, or Repeal, Amendment. Prohibition was dead —although a number of states, counties and cities have continued to maintain full or partial bans on liquor. "The adoption of the twenty-first amendment," said President Franklin D. Roosevelt in his first State of the Union message on January 3, 1934, "should give material aid to the elimination of those new forms of crime which came from the illegal traffic in liquor."

The well-intentioned experiment had not only cost the United States more than a billion dollars a year in lost taxes and import duties and deprived millions of Americans of a pleasure not evil in itself, but it also had another far-reaching effect—it furnished the first ideal training ground for racketeering and organized crime. The narcotics and vice trade, underway even before repeal, learned many survival and operating techniques from the experience with prohibition.

The temperance movement may also have worked against itself when it warped the true meaning of temperance and became top-heavy with extremists who, for fifteen years, were able to keep their ideas of morality hanging over the heads of the vast majority of the people. Had they the good sense to stick to any standard dictionary definition of temperance as "moderation in action, thought or feeling," or the open minds to respect the views of others about a matter that does not lend itself easily to enforcement, they might have done much to further the goal of responsible drinking behavior.

Two

Abuse and Use

◆·◆

NEIL: I can usually drink about eight to ten beers. After that I'm wiped out. I get drunk only once every weekend.

SHEILA: Alcohol isn't bad if you don't abuse it. I've seen people who have a lot, and I hate seeing adults drink. When I was little, I remember seeing my best friend's mother lying on the living room couch, totally out of it. I used to see her going to the package store, too. But funny that when I see kids my own age doing it, it doesn't bother me. I like to drink every so often, and sometimes it's fun getting a buzz, but what I hate is coming home dizzy, lying down in bed and getting the spins. Now that I'm eighteen, it's so much more comfortable, and I'm not scared or tense thinking that someone is going to find out.

◆·◆

Prohibition left its scars, and not all were from the bullets that flew during the gangland wars of the era. The attempt by biased groups to regulate personal habits by forcing a law that had no public support may well have left its mark in the attitudes of many people toward drinking, attitudes that have been passed down from parents to their children. For just as the restrictions of Prohibition incited a strong youthful rebellion against a foolish experiment and probably helped mold hundreds of thousands of problem drinkers, so, too, did sudden relaxation of the regulations probably contribute to abuse.

There are, of course, many reasons why people drink, and also drink too much, too often; some of these will be examined in the pages ahead. And while it would be simplistic to say that Prohibition or extreme permissiveness are at the root of the problems of alcohol abuse, the fact remains that both are important to consider.

Restriction of freedom, on the one hand, and a hang-loose philosophy on the other, each affects the way we conduct ourselves. And equally as important, they prevent us from learning what constitutes responsible drinking behavior. Telling people they must not and cannot drink because it represents a moral failing or because it will ruin health often only makes drinking more alluring, human nature being what it is. The vast majority of us, aware that the nonexcessive use of alcohol does not damage a healthy individual and, indeed, may even be beneficial, would shun such advice. We might also react too harshly to the advice and drink copiously, so intent might we be on doing what we consider to be right. So it might go with the individual who is guided by the "eat, drink and be merry for tomorrow we die" philosophy. Between the position of the Prohibitionist, who simply says "No," and the freewheeler, who says "Yes," there is the more sensible approach of, "Yes, if you choose, but . . ." And it is the "but" that will keep reappearing throughout this book when the discussion turns to drinking behavior. For, since drinking is very much a part of our culture and that of peoples throughout the world, it behooves us to do it sensibly—if we opt to drink. And by the same token, we must respect the choice of those who feel they can do without it.

It is also vital that we understand how alcohol works in the body, how drinking affects behavior, what some of the causes of alcoholism are believed to be, and what treatment is available for those unfortuate to be addicted. There are too many wrong ideas about alcohol. Righting some of these will clarify the subject of drinking and thereby aid in making the right choice; getting rid of the myths will also enable those who have a drinking problem to recognize the early warning signals, to stop denying it, and to seek help.

The majority of Americans, including young people, drink at least occasionally, and fortunately most do it without causing trouble for themselves or those with whom they live and work. Despite the fact that the key element in what they drink—ethyl alcohol, or ethanol—is an addicting drug that can dramatically affect the central nervous system and cause physiological changes, they handle it remarkably well and do not become alcoholics. They drink moderately, rarely are drunk and do not depend on alcohol to get them through life.

Before going any further, some definitions are in order. Bearing in mind that definitions in the area of human behavior are not as firm as those that apply, say, to mathematics or grammar, but often reflect the opinion of the person who gave them to us, consider these:

Alcoholism: There are hundreds of definitions of this complex illness that affects millions of Americans and costs the nation more than $25 billion a year. The World Health Organization, taking note of the different types of alcoholism which vary tremendously from one culture to the next, has defined alcoholism as a "chronic, behavioral disorder, marked by repeated drinking of alcohol in excess of the dietary and social customs of the community and to an extent that it interferes with the drinker's health or how he functions socially or economically." Another broad definition, given by the American Medical Association, runs as follows: "Alcoholism is an illness characterized by preoccupation with alcohol and loss of control over its consumption, such as to lead usually to intoxication if drinking; by chronicity; by progression; and by a tendency toward relapse. It is typically associated with physical disability and impaired emotional, occupational and/or social adjustments as a direct consequence of persistent excessive use." The AMA adds: "In short, alcoholism is regarded as a type of drug dependence of pathological extent and pattern, which ordinarily interferes seriously with the patient's total health and his adaptation to his environment." Put another way, alcoholism may be defined

27

simply as "a disease in which alcohol interferes with the physical, emotional and social well-being of an individual." Or, as "drinking that infringes on health, job, marriage and friendship or family relationships," according to a recent article on the subject in *Modern Medicine.*

Alcoholics also have been defined in various ways, among them: "One who drinks alcohol to the point that it interferes with some or all of the everyday aspects of life." Or, as "those excessive drinkers whose dependence upon alcohol has attained such a degree that it shows a noticeable interference with their physical and mental health, their interpersonal relations and their smooth social and economic function." Someone else has defined the alcoholic as a person who quits bragging and starts to lie about how much he or she drinks. The Rutgers Center of Alcohol Studies offers this: "An alcoholic is one who is unable to consistently choose whether he shall drink or not and who, if he drinks, is usually unable to consistently choose whether he shall stop nor not." (Loss of control over the consumption of liquor, not to be confused with drunkenness which is the *temporary* loss of control over physical and mental powers due to overconsumption, is a key element in alcoholism. It refers to the inability to stop drinking once it has started.) One last definition of an alcoholic: *Time* magazine recently quoted Mrs. Fred Tooze, head of the National Woman's Christian Temperance Union, as saying that an alcoholic is "anyone who drinks alcohol. As soon as they start to drink, they're on that road downward." *Time* added: "By that definition, many of the researchers in alcoholism would be practicing alcoholics themselves."

Problem Drinking: There is a fine line between the problem drinker (also called alcohol dependent) and the full-fledged alcoholic, and it may be impossible to arrive at any solid definition, just as it is difficult to draw a hard and firm line between the social, casual drinker and the problem drinker. (It is important to know, however, that the amount of liquor consumed, while a factor, is not the sole clue in any of the categories. Although alcoholism and problem drinking cannot occur without alcohol, alcohol alone can no more be blamed for causing the problems than marriage can be for causing divorce, sugar for causing diabetes, or the tubercle bacillus alone for causing tuberculosis. As often occurs, some alcoholics actually drink less liquor than do some so-called social drinkers.) In its 1974 report to Congress, the National Institute on Alcohol Abuse and Alcoholism (NIAAA) observed that problem drinking was thought to include such features as frequent intoxication and "binge" drinking—drinking heavily only at certain times—exhibition of certain signs attributed to physical dependence and loss of control, psychological dependence, disruption of normal social behavior patterns, including problems with spouse or relations, friends, neighbors, employers and police. (Physical dependence refers to the process whereby the body adapts to a drug and requires more and more of it to produce the physical and behavioral effects. When deprived of the drug, there are violent physical withdrawal symptoms, such as delirium tremens, the D.T.s, which occur when alcohol is suddenly withdrawn. Psychological dependence is what keeps the drug abuser enslaved by his or her habit. It is an emotional or mental adaptation to the effects of the drug, and the abuser requires its continued use to satisfy emotional and personality needs. A person so addicted leans on the drug to escape from reality, from problems and frustrations. It is the psychological factor that forces an addict who has been withdrawn from his physical dependence to return to drug abuse.) Alcohol, like heroin, causes strong psychological and physical dependence; increasing amounts are needed to produce the same effect. However, in advanced stages of alcoholism, there often is a reverse tolerance, that is, the addict needs less alcohol than before to produce the desired effect. The reason for this is not fully understood, but it may be that brain damage caused by long-term abuse of alcohol is to blame.

In broad terms, problem drinking—which may plague some thirty million Americans, many of them teenagers— can be defined as drinking enough to cause trouble for oneself or for society. The common factor in all drinking problems is the negative effect they have on the health or well-being of the drinker, and on his or her associates. The following criteria identify someone with a drinking problem: drinking in order to function or to cope with life, drinking frequently to intoxication, going to work or school intoxicated, driving while drunk, injuring oneself severely while drunk, getting into trouble with the law because of intoxication, gulping drinks for effect, marked personality and behavior changes after one or more drinks, doing, while under the influence of alcohol, anything the drinker says he would never do unless he or she were under the influence. It should be obvious from the foregoing that one does not need to progress to alcoholism—loss of self-control, or addiction, in the use of intoxicating beverages—to be adversely affected by drinking. Bearing in mind that each case is different and that the lines that divide the types of drinking behavior are often blurred, these are some of the typical warning signals of alcoholism: frequent and obvious intoxication, a steady increase in the amount of liquor consumed, tremors which signal brain damage, repeatedly expressing the need for a drink, often drinking alone or in the morning or when a crisis arises, frequent denial of drinking and annoyance when the subject is discussed, missing work regularly, particularly after weekends and holidays, hiding liquor, a history of arrests for drinking and driving, and the occurrence of blackouts—a period of temporary amnesia during which the person is fully conscious, walking and talking, but cannot recall it later. It is not "passing out," but a period of memory loss.

Social Drinking: The social drinker may or may not be a moderate drinker. Again, it is difficult to come up with a good definition, but one that has been accepted for moderate drinking goes back a hundred years to the British physician Francis Anstie who set up the "safe" limit: about three ounces of whiskey, or a half bottle of wine, or four glasses of beer a day, taken only with meals. In 1925, some American insurance firms accepted Anstie's limit as a guide when considering applications for life insurance policies. Dr. Morris E. Chafetz, director of the NIAAA, recently suggested that possibly the nation might experience fewer alcohol problems if Anstie's limit were adopted by those who choose to drink. He added, however, that tolerance does vary widely from person to person as well as in one individual according to circumstances.

The social drinker might be one who tailors drinking to the pattern of those around him or her or to the situation. There may be a cocktail or two before dinner, or once in a while before lunch. But, more often than not, the social drinker tries to avoid noontime imbibing. The social drinker may become intoxicated at times, but usually only at social functions such as weddings, parties or New Year's Eve celebrations. Heavy social drinkers have been called "social alcoholics." Individuals in this category may consume excessive quantities of alcohol and seek out social functions in order to drink; but they usually do not miss work, and their marriages generally do not suffer. While the "social alcoholic" may not be a true alcoholic, the pattern might serve as a springboard if the right combination of circumstances comes into play—as is true about any form of drinking.

Excessive Drinking: A special word of caution about this definition because a value judgment is involved. It is true, of course, that heavy drinking can cause numerous problems for both drinkers and their associates—a high incidence of automobile accidents, for example—but what is considered excessive for one individual or in one situation may not be in another. It has been said that one person's blizzard is another's ski trip, and this applies to the term excessive drinking, which may be defined as drinking more than is considered normal in a given society, but can be stopped when the drinker becomes aware of the danger ahead. It must be said that simply counting the number of glasses or bottles emptied is of little help in understanding the causes of the alcoholism or the effects of alcohol on both mind and body, for in many localities there is a low intake of alcohol, but a high alcoholism rate. Sweden, for example, which has had one of the lowest rates of consumption, has a high incidence of alcoholism. As one investigator put it in the *Quarterly Journal of Studies on Alcohol*: "Although heavy daily quantity appears to imply a degree of drinking that is abnormal, and likely to lead to physical and psychosocial dependence on alcohol, it cannot be assumed that this will inevitably occur, particularly in communities where heavy daily consumption of alcoholic beverages, particularly in the form of wine, is normal practice." In France, it was once advised, "No more than a liter of wine a day." However, many alcoholics average less than that, while some social drinkers consume more.

If any definition holds firm, it is that alcoholism is an illness, a treatable one, just as schizophrenia or TB are; the alcoholic and problem drinker are not sinners or criminals to be denounced from the pulpit or locked in a cell, nor should such individuals be used as often as they are by rather shallow standup comedians who see them only as material for their mindless jokes. There is nothing at all comical about a middle-aged woman on skid row, thrown out by her husband, guzzling cheap wine from a bottle hidden in a paper bag; or, at her worst, drinking paint thinner or shaving lotion or bootleg Jamaica ginger, 83 percent alcohol, the ticket to a cut-rate high and, two weeks later, paralysis of the legs and hands. Nor about the young surgeon who drinks before an operation to steady his nerves, or the executive who quaffs vodka and orange juice in the morning, a bracer in the men's room at the office, two or three martinis for lunch, one before he boards the commuter train, two before supper, wine with his meals and a nightcap or two before he falls into bed to sleep through to the next workday. And neither is there anything funny about the teenager who downs a six-pack of beer as though it were soda while sitting in his car, then takes off in a stupor, can in one hand, wheel in the other, until he runs into a tree or another human being.

But again, it cannot be emphasized too strongly that while the potential for this sort of behavior may be in all of us, the majority consumes alcohol with no adverse effects. As the NIAAA report put it: "Alcohol alone may not cause health or social problems, even in a universally drinking society, and the type of drink may not matter as much as the patterns and purposes of drinking."

There are, of course, many individuals for whom even one drink would begin the chain reaction—one drink followed by another and on to oblivion. A Japanese proverb says it well: "First the man takes a drink, then the drink takes a drink, then the drink takes the man." These people can never learn to drink responsibly. But not everyone who drinks is or will become an alcoholic or a problem drinker. Not so long as the individual who chooses to drink understands the difference between healthy and unhealthy patterns of drinking, knows how to avoid the pattern that will lead to alcoholism, is aware of the warning signs and takes time to learn some basic facts about alcohol and its effects on the body.

"The public suffers from much ignorance concerning alcohol and from ambivalent feelings toward it," the NIAAA report found. "Worse yet, heavier drinkers know less about alcohol than do light drinkers or abstainers. In general, American attitudes about drinking are marked by confusion and dissent."

All of you have gone with parents or friends to a restaurant, and before you even settle into your chairs, the waiter approaches, pad in hand, and asks, "What can I get you to drink?" or "Would you like a cocktail?" Almost never, unless the place doesn't have a liquor license, do the patrons get asked if they'd like a drink—of tomato or apple juice, tea, lemonade or some other non-alcoholic beverage before the meal. Many of you have also watched your father and mother at the door, greeting friends for a party; almost as routinely and quickly as the waiter, they ask, "What would you like to drink?" meaning, everyone knows, "Do you prefer beer, wine or liquor?" Some people will accept with, "Whatever you're having," or they'll be specific about a brand of whiskey or a type of drink. Only a few will decline anything, or ask for a light wine or a glass of soda or ice water.

To illustrate how drinking is so intermixed with our culture, the story is told of a Sunday school class putting on a nativity play for Christmas. None of the children wanted to portray the rather villainous role of the innkeeper who refused lodging to Joseph. At last, one six-year-old boy agreed to take the part but during the performance, after he dutifully told Joseph there was no room in the inn, he added on his own: "But please come in and have a drink."

We also have our "social hours," "happy hours," "champagne breakfasts," "Bloody Mary brunches." We are bombarded with full-color magazine advertisements featuring tranquil or seductive male-female scenes at home or outdoors, accompanied by such lines as: "To end the day, or start the evening. To share with friends, at a party or with a friend, alone." "So you may enjoy this rare pleasure wherever in the world you may be." "Follow the golden eagles to Imperial pleasure." "Distilled and brought to perfection in every bottle of J & B rare Scotch." "The smooth, satisfying flavor that has made this the world's favorite bottle of Scotch." "The place: on the top of the world. The mood: elegant. The drink: Kahlau Black Russian." "Spend a week with the white rum martini: Let its smoothness grow on you. You'll wind up having the best relationship anyone ever had with a martini."

Then there are the enticing names for drinks, appealing to every taste and social station: orange blossom, fogcutter, pink lady, stinger, screwdriver, bullshot, brandy Alexander, and boilermaker. "May I freshen that?" a host or hostess will ask. "Is the punch spiked?" a preteen wants to know.

"I'll have one for the road," announces the last to leave the party, the individual with the "hollow leg" who, "the morning after," belts down a "hair of the dog" for the "hangover" that has descended. Finally, there is the special language of denial. Just as we use synonyms to mask the words death and die, so, too, do we attempt to hide the stigma of being drunk, using expressions borrowed from the drug culture or phrases our parents or theirs used: "bombed," "wasted," "tight," "high," "lit," "plastered," "plowed," "stoned," "soused," "three sheets to the wind," "clobbered," "blind," "gonzo," "smashed," "potted," "stinking," "blotto" and "shit-faced."

Drinking, then, is widespread, ingrained in our language, our work, our play and our customs. The United States, in fact, outranks all but one of the twenty-four other countries from which reports are available on per capita consumption of distilled spirits. Between 1960 and 1970, per capita consumption of alcohol in this country increased 26 percent, to 2.6 gallons of straight alcohol per adult per year. Retail sales of alcohol in 1971 were $24.2 billion and have increased yearly. This contrasts with $2 billion expended for prescribed psychoactive drugs and an estimated $2 billion for illegal drugs. That year, Americans drank a record high of four and a half billion gallons of beer, wine and liquor.

But despite that quantity and given the aforementioned problems of definition, it is difficult to say with any accuracy how many users and abusers of alcohol there actually are. Several national surveys have shown that more than half—one survey puts the percentage at 68 percent—of all American adults drink at least occasionally. This would figure out to at least 100 million people. (The adult classification includes those eighteen and over.) With regard to how much people drink, one Harris survey covering 1972 to 1974 classified 9 percent as heavy drinkers, 18 percent as moderate, 31 percent as light and 42 percent as abstainers and infrequent drinkers. (The latter category included those who drink less than once a month or not at all.)

Estimating the number of alcoholics and problem drinkers is also difficult in view of the variety of definitions and the fact that many of those who have a difficult time with drinking either lie about their habits or fail to realize they have a problem. "The number of Americans whose

34

lives alcohol has adversely affected depends on definition," said the NIAAA report. "Those under active treatment for alcoholism by public or private agencies are probably in the upper hundreds of thousands, but there may be as many as 10 million people whose drinking has created some problem for themselves or their families or friends or employers, or with the police within the past year." Temperance groups, of course, along with alcoholics themselves, feel the figures may be too low; others, suspicious of the statistics and how they are arrived at, maintain they are too high, purposely inflated, even, to drum up popular support for congressional pressure for more funding to fight the problem.

But whatever the true incidence, there is little doubt that those who are afflicted with the disease—and the classic skid row alcoholic represents only about 3 to 5 percent of the total—are part of a national tragedy. For alcohol abuse can shorten life ten to fifteen years, harm the infants of alcoholic mothers, has been implicated in the development of certain cancers and is a factor in half the murders and a fourth of the suicides in the United States. In 1971, violent crimes associated with alcohol and the so-called 100 percent alcohol-related offenses (such as drunkenness, disorderly conduct, vagrancy and driving under the influence) accounted for 3.6 million arrests, or 41 percent of all arrests. The cost to the nation's criminal justice system of violent and antisocial behavior associated with alcohol misuse was more than a half billion dollars that year.

Based on data supplied by the National Highway Traffic Safety Administration, alcohol misuse contributed to 43 percent of the nonpedestrian traffic fatalities (19,000 deaths) in 1971; 38 percent of the adult pedestrian fatalities (2,700 deaths); 14 percent of the personal injury accidents, and 6.8 percent of the property damage accidents. Thus, about 40 percent (21,700) of the motor vehicle deaths were believed attributable to alcohol in 1971.

Alcohol abuse also plays a part in some ten thousand accidental deaths a year at home and on the job and makes the abuser seven times more likely than the non-abuser to be divorced or separated. According to government statistics, the largest single area of economic loss, $9.35 billion, is the lost production of goods and services that can be attributed to the reduced productivity of alcohol-troubled male workers. Furthermore, treatment for alcohol-related conditions accounted for more than 12 percent of the $68.3 billion health bill for adult Americans in 1971. Alcohol and alcoholism probably also contribute to many deaths and serious conditions that are attributed to other causes by physicians who, in an effort to spare the feelings of survivors or the patient, neglect to note "alcoholism" on the death certificate or hospital record.

There is little doubt also that alcoholism and alcohol abuse continue unabated and, in fact, appear to be increasing in frequency, particularly among the age group at whom this book is aimed, and among women.

Let's look first at teenage drinking, which involves mostly beer and the fruit-flavored pop wines. A number of studies indicate that a high proportion of teenagers drink—anywhere from 71 to 92 percent of high school students having at least tried alcohol beverages. Among seventh graders, another survey found, the indication is that 63 percent of boys and 54 percent of girls have tried alcohol. The average young person, in fact, has first tasted alcohol, probably an experimental sip, by age ten. Furthermore, it is not only believed that alcohol use is increasing among that age group, but that it is replacing marijuana as the drug of choice of people under twenty-one. Says Dr. Chafetz: "Youth of today are reverting to their parents' value systems. Along with the return of the fraternity, proms and all that." (That may be true but many teenagers use both marijuana and alcohol.)

But, with the switch from pot to booze, and despite the sighs of relief from many parents to the effect that "at least our child isn't on dope," has come the increase in problem drinking among youth. It has been estimated that 36 percent of high school students report getting drunk at least four times a year. At the 1974 annual meeting of the Canadian Paediatric Society, Dr. Norman M. Wolfish expressed the belief that alcohol addiction had increased alarmingly to the point where one percent of all sixteen-year-olds in the United States and Canada are "desperate, chronic alcoholics." He added: "Young persons have turned to the old, reliable, easily obtainable and socially acceptable panacea of all ills, alcohol. Alcohol accounts for more drug use than all other drugs combined."

In a recent survey of public high school students by the New York City Addiction Services Agency, it was found that 26 percent of the students drink alcohol two or three times a week or regularly on weekends. "Alcohol, particularly wine," said one official, "is cheaper to buy than drugs. Parents who drink themselves are more tolerant of the alcohol habit among their children than of drugs."

Alcohol misuse among young people is not confined to the United States. Social welfare officials in Bonn, West Germany, report cases of addiction among children as young as ten. In Stuttgart, according to a Reuters news report, quoting a social worker, "There is hardly a school where, during break periods, or even during lessons, some form of alcohol is not handed around."

Against this background of abuse, it is tempting to assume that drinking among youth breeds alcoholism along with delinquent behavior quickly and surely. With regard to the first part of that statement, there is no proof that early exposure to alcohol will lead, by itself, to excessive drinking or alcohol abuse later in life. For just as the number of alcoholics in the overall population does not constitute anywhere near a majority of drinkers, so, too, is the number of young people in *real* trouble, or destined for trouble, with alcohol a relatively small one. The potential for abuse, of course, is always present, but it is not the mere presence of alcohol or the number of people who drink that is important. It is *how* and *why* people drink that are important. Again Dr. Chafetz:

Studies do not indicate that our youth are in more massive danger of developing alcohol problems than their elders, nor that the clarion calls of the doom-seekers must be issued against the youth of today. My impression is that the vast majority of the present young generation will burgeon into responsible adulthood. Yet, who can deny that we live in tense, anxious, frightening times. New conflicts arise before the old ones are resolved. Alcohol use, if not properly faced, may well lead to problems of increased magnitude. At NIAAA, our philsophy is that alcoholism, like many other illnesses, lends itself to many types of preventive measures.

With reference to the relationship between driving and delinquency, it should be remembered that it is not easy to predict responses to alcohol. Psychological, environmental physical and hereditary factors are at work when a problem with alcohol develops, just as they are in creating the problems that fall under the heading of mental illness. Some studies have found the percentage of alcohol users among delinquents to be the same as among "normal" high school students—with the difference being in not how many of each group drink but in *how* they drink. Other studies conclude that while drinking may well be more widespread among troublesome youths, it is not the drinking that is to blame for the delinquency but the fact that the young person who finds it difficult to get along in society, with his or her friends and relatives, seeks out situations and an environment which supports the drinking.

Commenting on problems associated with teenage drinking, the NIAAA report noted that where the incidence of "deviant drinking" has been shown to be decidedly higher among juvenile delinquents than among members of the general population, there is the suggestion that "those who are anti-social or maladjusted misbehave typically in a variety of ways, one of which is over-drinking."

A number of investigators, then, see adolescent problem drinking as one of a class of behaviors, commonly referred to as antisocial, that involve the potential for getting into trouble. They do not see it as something that stands by itself, apart from other forms of deviant behavior. One personality study of junior and senior high school students revealed that those with a drinking problem did not value achievement as much as nonproblem drinkers; problem drinkers were also much more tolerant of deviant behavior. Problem drinker girls were found to be less compatible with their parents, while both sexes who had a drinking problem were supportive of drinking by adolescents.

Turning to alcohol consumption among women, it has long been believed that more men than women were alcoholics. Until the 1950s, according to the National Institute of Mental Health, there were five or six male alcoholics in the United States for every female alcoholic. In the 1960s, the estimated ratio dropped to four to one, and today the proportion is nearing, if it is not already there, fifty-fifty. (In Dade County, Florida, nearly half of the reported seventy-eight thousand alcoholics are women.) There are several ways of looking at this increase. One is that with more and more job equality and freedom come additional stresses, and these may well be leading to more drinking among women. Women can now drink in bars that were traditionally for men only without being branded as social outcasts. Some psychologists feel that the added strains of this new life-style might push a susceptible woman over the edge into a drinking problem, just as a man who is too weak to stand the stress of competing and performing might be pushed. Newly visible, such a woman—who might have been able to hide her drinking problem at home in years past—is forced, either by her employer or her own embarrassment, to seek treatment. Another view is that women, even at home, have always drunk, often to excess, but nursed their habit alone, shielded by a sympathetic or embarrassed family and friends—who often prevented her from seeking the help she desperately needed. (The five to one ratio of male to female alcoholics was based on the number of women who attended clinics.) But now that the whole subject of alcoholism needn't be a source of shame more women are willing to face up to their drinking problem and are seeking help and undergoing treatment.

The NIAAA report noted that among junior and senior high school students, girls drink less than boys, with drinking becoming more frequent with increasing age. "The use of alcohol among girls has approached that of boys," the report said, "though the proportion of girls who drink at least every week is smaller."

Along these lines it is interesting to note that in 1975, the Medical Foundation, the research and community health agency of the United Way of Massachusetts Bay, found in a survey that teenage girls rivaled boys in drinking and exceeded them in the use of drugs at one of the Boston area's schools, Brookline High. A previous survey, conducted in 1971, showed the girls to be behind the boys in drinking to intoxication and in other drug use. The new study also found that the high school girls were drinking hard liquor more often, while the boys generally stayed with beer and wine. One reason for the change, according to a school official, may be the increase in advertising depicting beautiful women drinking.

Aside from sex and age, there are other factors associated with use and misuse of alcohol. Among them are ethnic background, religion, educational levels, socioeconomic status, occupation and place of residence. One should not, however, blame these things for problem drinking. That would be too simple, as well as erroneous, as we will see later on when we discuss why people drink and the causes of alcoholism. Nevertheless, whether one drinks or not often does reflect the above factors, for all of us are strongly affected by intimate contacts with other people, and we tend to play the roles that have been mapped out for us by them. Our attitudes and our behavior, then, are learned as well as inherited. Mormons, for example, are forbidden to use alcohol, but the Camba Indians of Bolivia engage in explosive drinking bouts on weekends with the approval of their culture; other primitive societies drink heavily at harvest or at spring planting time.

Let's look at some of these factors that play a part in whether and how much a person drinks, keeping in mind that drinkers may be found where drink is forbidden or uncommon, and nondrinkers where the habit is rampant.

Country of Origin. "Among Americans of Irish extraction," wrote sociologists Mabel A. Elliott of Pennsylvania College for Women and Francis E. Merrill of Dartmouth in their book, *Social Disorganization,*

> a strong cultural tradition persists that drinking and conviviality are inseparable companions and that hard liquor offers the fastest road to a pleasant euphoria. There is a notion among the Irish that virility is at least partially measured by the amount of liquor the male can consume and still walk. This tradition is often shared by many Americans whose ancestors came from northern Europe and Scandinavia. An unusually heavy incidence of alcoholism is apparent among the descendants of immigrants from these countries. The Italian-Americans, on the other hand, have a tradition of serving alcoholic beverages with meals and exhibit no such pronounced tendency to overindulgence. The Jewish people have a strong cultural antipathy to alcohol and show an extraordinary immunity to alcoholism and the alcoholic psychoses. . . . The tendency to drink to excess is not in any sense a racial or inherited trait. The social forces that produce a high percentage of alcoholism are not based on biological differences.

Some of this may still hold true, but habits do change over generations and with the times. In Italy, for instance,

40

according to the World Health Organization (WHO), the quantity of alcohol consumed more than doubled between 1941 and 1961. At the same time, the number of first admissions to hospitals for mental illness connected with excessive consumption of alcohol tripled from 1947 to 1962. And this in a country that is often cited as one where alcohol consumption was consistently high with almost no medical problems.

In Japan, health authorities have devoted a good deal of attention to the growing incidence of alcoholism and other problems of drinking since World War II. "The rising standard of living and, especially in urban areas," observes WHO, "the weakening of ties that bound the individual to a closely integrated traditional structure seem to have given rise to the type of 'symptomatic drinking'—drinking that uses alcohol as a drug to escape from the pressures of personal and interpersonal conflicts—prevalent in some Western countries."

Of the role of ethnic background in U.S. drinking habits, the NIAAA has this to say:

> Alcoholism and problem drinking rates tend to be low among groups whose drinking habits are well integrated with the rest of their culture. It is, therefore, not surprising that ethnic background and generational status are important determinants of drinking patterns in the U.S. It has been reported that Irish-Americans have more trouble with problem drinking than other American groups of the same social class, that little of their drinking is associated with important rituals and that intoxication is often deliberately sought. Italian-Americans, on the other hand, have strong sanctions against drunkenness, apply little social pressure to participate in drinking, and usually consume alcohol with meals.

First generation Italian-Americans, the report goes on, drink frequently but have few alcohol-related problems, but later generations have higher rates of heavy drinking. One recent survey of first generation Irish-Americans and their descendants, and Italian-Americans and theirs, has shown that the first generation Italian-Americans generally confine themselves to drinking wine daily; later generations, however, do not. Though distilled spirits consumption is higher among the first generation Italian-Americans than among Italians in Italy, they drink spirits more moderately than later generations. The Italian-Americans also drink more often than Irish-Americans, the surveys have found, but the latter take five or six drinks—regardless of beverage type—on a single occasion more often than the Italian-Americans.

Religion. As noted, a number of religious groups, as well as persons of no particular religious persuasion, regard drinking alcoholic beverages as unhealthy, antisocial, immoral or sinful. It naturally follows that when total abstinence is the accepted norm in a group, there is relatively little, if any, alcoholism. Other religious groups permit their members to use alcoholic beverages socially as well as in ceremonies such as Holy Communion in which wine is drunk. Still others might restrict the use of wines or liquor to ceremonies or customs—toasts at weddings, or drinking at a wake for the dead.

A national survey of American drinking practices, done in 1969 by the Rutgers Center for Alcohol Studies, found there were relatively high proportions of drinkers and heavy drinkers among Catholics. Jews had the lowest number of abstainers of the three major American religions. They also had a very high proportion of light drinkers and the lowest proportion of heavy drinkers. So-called liberal Protestants demonstrated a pattern somewhat similar to the Catholics, although there were fewer heavy drinkers; conservative Protestants had the largest proportion of abstainers and the lowest proportion of heavy drinkers when the four groups were compared. (Later surveys have indicated an increase in both light and moderate drinking among Jew and Catholics.) Still another survey, a 1974 study of Irish-American and Italian-American drinking practices, linked frequency of use of alcohol to the church attendance of both groups. Those who attended church more often were more likely to report infrequent drinking. Also, the more frequent the church attendance, the less alcohol was consumed per occasion. This was true of both ethnic groups. Catholics and liberal Protestants, as well as those who do not attend church, also have been shown to be problem drinkers more often than other religious groups.

It should be pointed out here that persons brought up in an abstinent society occasionally rebel and become problem drinkers, and when this occurs the drinker usually

42

becomes guilty over his or her breach of the law of the group. Such guilt may worsen the drinking problem as the individual begins to drink more and more to blot out the guilt.

Education and Social Status. Most authorities believe that the amount of education is closely linked to whether a person drinks and how much is consumed. A 1963 survey published in the *Quarterly Journal of Studies on Alcohol* found that in general the proportion of those who drink was highest among those with higher education, income and vocational status. And while problem drinking may be found among those with more or less education, and among both those with low and high social status, the indication is that there are more abstainers among those with less than an eighth grade education—and more abstainers than drinkers in the lower socioeconomic levels. There is ample statistical evidence to show also that the number of heavy drinkers increases as the educational level rises, as does both moderate and heavy drinking with a rise in social class.

Insofar as problem drinking is concerned, however, studies conducted in the 1960s indicate that problem drinkers were often, among other things, poor men under twenty-five. Data such as this suggest that the drinker in a group in which drinking is not prevalent—lower education or lower social scale—may be the most likely to encounter trouble with police or society because of that drinking. Another word about social class: Those at the top of the scale do not regard drinking as a moral problem, which it is not per se. The upper middle class shares that view. Members of the lower middle class, more rigid in their scruples and religious convictions, feel they are more "respectable" than those beneath them and tend to take a more judgmental position with regard to heavy drinking; those lowest on the scale, trapped as often as they are in poor housing and infrequent or dead-end work, often drink to excess to deaden their mental anguish, or to give them the false courage to hold up a store or assault those who are wealthier.

With regard to wealth, the University of Michigan Institute for Social Research found in 1973 that the wealthier in a national survey increased their regular use of alcohol by 21 percent after high school, compared to a 5 percent increase among the poorer. And a study in the *British*

Journal of Addictions reported in 1971 that in the Toronto junior and senior high school students surveyed, alcohol use was highest among children whose fathers were professionals or managers.

Occupation and Residence. "Sociological influences may derive from such diverse but related considerations as occupational or geographic proximity and pride," according to the American Medical Association's 1967 *Manual on Alcoholism*, published for physicians. "Consider the brewery worker who often has immediate access to beer and whose capacity for the beverage he helps produce is his mark of personal prestige. People who live in wine country, where life is almost entirely oriented to, and economically dependent on, the vineyard and its produce will take greater interest in using and promoting these products than will others. Not only is wine usually more available there, but its use is enthusiastically endorsed." France and Spain are good examples of this. France, where wine is pretty much a way of life, records 34.8 deaths per one hundred thousand each year from cirrhosis, an inflammatory disease of the liver. Spain, also a large wine producer, has 13 percent of the world's alcoholics. "The temptation to drink is hard to resist in this wine-oriented country in which the sales of hard liquors, like brandy and whiskey, are on the rise," says a report in a recent issue of *Medical Tribune*. "Minimal taxes on beverages make it cheaper to drink in Spain than in most countries; wine is cheaper than water in some villages, and local brandy is cheaper than coffee in many bars in the big cities."

It is true that what one does for a living, white-collar or blue-collar work, has something to do with the pattern of drinking. Cocktail parties, Saturday night beer busts, martini lunches, wine and cheese parties, hard cider and square dance "socials," highballs at the enlisted men's or officers' clubs, moonshine whiskey in a shack in the hills, International Night at American Legion or Elks or Eagles halls—all attract special customers who tend to drink in groups organized according to occupational status if not by actual job (regular meetings of real estate dealers, physicians or teachers).

Farm owners, it turns out, appear to have the lowest proportion of drinkers and heavy drinkers, while professionals and businessmen in the city have the highest. A 1972 army study indicated that both officers and enlisted men drink more than civilians of the same age, that officers get less into trouble because of their drinking than do civilians, but that enlisted men get into considerably more difficulty than their civilian counterparts.

The region of the country and degree of urban living may also influence drinking habits. A 1963 survey found that the proportion of those who drink at all was highest in the Middle Atlantic and New England states, and lowest in the South Central states, and highest, also, among residents of larger communities of every region. The same survey indicated that the percentage of problem drinkers was highest in the western part of the United States and among residents of larger cities. It is interesting to note that according to the 1967 National Institute of Mental Health Report on Alcohol and Alcoholism, prominence given to apparent differences in reported rates of alcoholism in various cities and states "has provoked much regional embarrassment or pride, but the comparisons are not believed to be reliable."

One problem with linking liquor consumption to region is that some areas have a high rate of tourism and conventions, Las Vegas and Washington, D.C., for example, and the statistics would reflect that. Today, according to government statistics, there still are proportionately more drinkers in New England and the Middle Atlantic and Pacific coast states than elsewhere. However, the proportion of heavier drinkers may be increasing slightly in such traditionally "light" drinking areas as the Southeast and Mountain states, and is decreasing slightly in the coastal and Middle Atlantic regions. "It is difficult to determine whether these shifts may be due to real changes in individual drinking habits, or to the rather complex mobility patterns of the population as a whole," the NIAAA report noted. Also, residents of cities and towns have historically been more problem-prone than those who live in suburbs and rural areas, but new surveys indicate that such residential differences are disappearing. Those who register highest on the drinking scale are now found nearly equally in suburbs, cities and towns. Only those in the rural areas seem to have slightly lower rates of problems.

While all of the foregoing elements have something to do with drinking patterns, they should not be considered prime causes of alcoholism or problem drinking. Researchers are pursuing their studies of the causes—and there are many—of runaway drinking. The studies cover many areas, including environmental conditions, genetic and chemical abnormalities, emotional disorders and childhood deprivation.

Three

Causes of Alcoholism

$$\bullet\text{---}\bullet\bullet\text{---}\bullet$$

JOE: When I drink, I drink to feel good. Since I'm not old enough to buy it myself, it's not worthwhile to go to all the trouble you do to get it without at least being happy. When I get very depressed, I want a beer or two to put me in a good mood. When I drink, I don't have any more problems, I can laugh till I turn blue and it won't matter at all. I will drink beer only, anytime I can get it. It makes me feel like part of a fantasy, and I like that very much.

BETH: I just drink when I go out to bars, because my boyfriend plays in a band and I get my drinks half price. It doesn't take me much to get zippy. I think really drunk people are funny or obnoxious. I hate alcoholics and have no pity for anyone who gets that way. If I'm going to get fried, I mean really zonked, I like to do that with other people who will be just as bad off. That way, I don't get embarrassed, I don't stand out.

$$\bullet\text{---}\bullet\bullet\text{---}\bullet$$

People discovered alcohol's power a long time ago, and the reasons for drinking are many: to party, to celebrate, to improve appetite or add to the taste of meals, as part of religious ceremonies, to relax, to get drunk, to escape, for courage, to forget our worries.

46

Most adults, fortunately, drink in what is called an "integrative" way—using alcohol in conjunction with other activities such as meals or an evening with friends. Such people generally drink because they like to, because they enjoy the pleasurable feelings of relaxing and socializing that alcohol is capable of producing under the right circumstances.

Determining exactly where social drinking ends and problem drinking starts is, as we have said, most difficult, but it would seem that the further one moves from an integrative pattern the more at risk that person is of being nudged into the problem area, and from there possibly into a style of drinking whose key element is lack of control—drinking because the drinker must. For such people, alcohol is no longer a beverage to be sipped in moderation with food, friends and good conversation, no longer the social lubricant that induces a mild and pleasant sense of well-being, but a harsh and powerful potion that will never be drunk in a moderate way. These individuals are hooked, propped up by a fragile glass crutch. "Most alcoholics," observed one authority, "hate liquor, hate the taste, hate the result, hate themselves for succumbing, but they cannot stop."

Why does one become an alcoholic? Is there such an entity as an alcoholic personality? Can alcoholism be inherited? Why do people who choose to drink do so at all?

These are some of the questions that occupy psychiatrists and psychologists, biologists, sociologists and a host of other specialists. There are many theories, but few hard answers, and about all one can say with any degree of certainty is that alcohol by itself does not cause alcoholism. There also are no specific beverages that are responsible for alcohol addiction—one can be a beer or wine alcoholic as well as a hard liquor alcoholic. What a person chooses to drink is largely a matter of taste, cost, availability and custom.

Keeping in mind that alcoholism (of which there can be many forms) and drunkenness are essentially different problems, and that the best answer to cause probably lies in a complicated interaction of several factors, let's examine some of them. First, some of the physiological and biochemical factors.

Heredity, errors in the body's chemistry that prevent the alcoholic from using alcohol properly, brain defects, allergy, vitamin deficiency, glandular problems, a defective "thermostat" that causes an uncontrollable thirst for alcohol all have been examined by researchers. But thus far, none has been shown to be specifically responsible for alcoholism. There is no physical examination or blood test that can yet be performed to determine why a person has become an alcoholic, or whether he or she will become one; and no one has isolated a specific gene, that unit of heredity, for alcoholism. None of this means that these areas of research will always be dry holes, for there may well be some definitive physical or biological factor responsible; alcoholism could turn out to be due to some error in metabolism, the process whereby food is transformed into basic elements that can be used by the body for fuel and growth. Some researchers have suggested, for example, that excessive alcohol consumption may be the result of the body's decreased ability to utilize acetate, a salt that is normally produced during alcohol metabolism and is vital to many of the body's biochemical functions. Some scientists believe that because of this less than normal ability to use the salt, the alcoholic, requiring more of it, develops a strong "thirst" for alcohol which is the source of the salt. Alcoholism, then, would result from some metabolic system gone wrong, a malfunction that triggers the craving for alcohol.

Another research approach a few years ago suggested that alcohol addiction may be the same as morphine addiction, or very similar to it, and it may be caused by the formation of morphine or morphinelike drugs in the body. The difference in addiction may be only a matter of the length of time and dosage required to develop a dependence, according to evidence brought to light by the research group which made the suggestion reported in *Chemical and Engineering News*. The scientists, at the Veterans Administration Hospital in Houston, Texas, said that large quantities of alcohol in the body may inhibit the way dopamine, a body chemical involved in nerve transmission, works. Instead of performing in the normal way, the dopamine is converted into a chemical called THP, which is the intermediate chemical in poppies that leads to the biosynthesis of morphine. In laboratory animals, and presumably in human beings, THP may lead to the formation of morphine alkaloids, and to subsequent addiction, it was theorized.

It has also been suggested that alcoholism is caused by vitamin deficiencies, and researchers have been able to demonstrate that increased alcohol intake can be induced in experimental animals by such a lack. Animals, incidentally, appear to be more resistant to alcohol addiction than people, and this has hampered research on the disease to some extent. But there have been some notable successes in addicting animals such as beagles, monkeys and mice. At the University of North Carolina Medical School, a team of scientists administered daily doses of alcohol—equal to a fifth of 90-proof liquor a day—by stomach tube to monkeys and dogs. Later, the animals experienced the same withdrawal symptoms as humans: rigid and spastic muscle movements, convulsions, fear, tremors and even death.

In an experiment designed to learn more about vitamin deficiency and alcohol intake, a group of scientists deprived rats of vitamin B (the B-complex vitamins are required daily and are essential to growth and life) and found that the animals, when offered water or alcohol, chose the latter as a substitute for the necessary energy source. One of the suggestions that stemmed from such investigations was that if one has good nutrition from infancy there is less chance that he or she will become an alcoholic. However, it is often difficult to relate the results of animal studies to humans, and most of the nutritional shortages seen in serious cases of alcoholism appear to be a result of the disease rather than its cause. Other experiments have shown, in fact, that when vitamin-deprived rats are offered a third choice, a sugar solution, they choose that over the alcohol.

Allergy has been blamed for some cases of alcoholism, but so far there is no proof that the disorder is that kind of reaction because it has not been shown that alcoholics are generally allergic to liquor itself or to other components of alcoholic beverages. One study of alcoholics did demonstrate recently that they had more positive reactions to a number of foods than did ex-drinkers or nonalcoholics. But, it is believed that this indicated only that such sensitization to various foods may be a symptom tied to alcoholism, rather than proof of allergy to alcohol.

The role of heredity in alcoholism has been debated for years, with the believers pointing to the fact that the disease occurs frequently in the children of alcoholics.

Others offer equally strong evidence that it occurs often among the offspring of abstainers, too.

Inherited disorders are passed on through the genes, from parents to offspring. An example is the blood disorder hemophilia which is transmitted by females, who are not usually affected by it, to male offspring. Some people inherit a tendency toward certain diseases, as opposed to actually inheriting them. Such individuals begin life with a built-in weakness of some sort that makes them susceptible to a disorder. For example, we don't inherit allergies like hay fever; we may, on the other hand, develop a predisposition, or tendency, to become allergic. If both of our parents are allergic, or if there is allergy on both sides of the family, chances are that we will develop an allergy.

In the case of alcoholism, a number of studies have found that alcoholism is common in certain families, and that the children of alcoholics have significantly high rates of the disease. Dr. E. M. Jellinek, an authority on alcoholism, reported years ago that out of a total of 4,372 alcoholics, 52 percent had an alcoholic parent. Other studies indicate that if a person has an alcoholic parent the chances that that person will develop the disease is four times greater than that of the general population. It was Dr. Jellinek's conclusion, however, that rather than any direct hereditary transmission of alcoholism, it seemed that some people inherited a liability for developing infirmities —and that the infirmity in some takes the form of alcoholism. Predisposing factors, many believe, not a specific "alcoholic gene," make a person ripe for the development of alcoholism. The predisposing factor might simply be being born into the kind of environment that fosters alcoholic behavior, or an inherited biochemical defect that might affect the brain, creating drastic changes in personality and behavior that force the individual to turn to alcohol as a way out. Some people might inherit a certain physiological makeup that causes them to be either more susceptible to the effects of alcohol or more apt to handle it better, be it something wrong in genes or enzymes, or inherited body build, which is also a factor in how alcohol affects us. A few years ago, Dr. Allan A. Parry, chief of alcoholic services at Morristown Memorial Hospital in New Jersey, reported that alcoholics are born with a tendency to be biologically intolerant of alcohol. Exposure to liquor, he said, changes the structure of alcoholics' body cells, and their need for alcohol becomes compulsive. "What might be inherited," Dr. Donald Goodwin, psychiatrist at Washington University once suggested, "is how alcohol makes you feel. A large number of people could never become alcoholic because they are sensitive to alcohol—it gives them vertigo or makes them vomit. There are many others for whom alcohol doesn't do much emotionally and others who don't like the feeling of losing control."

In 1973, an American-Danish research team, among them Dr. Goodwin, reported a strong hereditary association with alcoholism. In their study, the group looked at fifty-five men who had been separated from their biological parents during early infancy. They were adopted by nonrelatives, but each of the men had at least one biological parent who had been hospitalized for alcoholism. The investigators compared the fifty-five men with seventy-eight other adopted men whose biological parents had no known history of alcoholism—and found that "significantly more" of the first group had a history of drinking problems and psychiatric treatment. Ten of the fifty-five children of an alcoholic parent were found to be alcoholic, four of the seventy-eight were whose parents were not.

"The data indicate that children of alcoholics are more likely to have alcoholic problems than are children of non-alcoholics," the researchers reported in the *Archives of General Psychiatry*, "despite being separated from their alcoholic parents early in life." They emphasized however, that genetic predisposition "remains more probable than proved and certainly may not apply to all alcoholics."

There is, of course, a delicate balance between heredity and environment, but many researchers today lean heavily toward the idea that alcoholism is related more to environment than to genetics. In the 1940s, Dr. Anne Roe of Harvard conducted studies than ran counter to the notion of a hereditary basis for alcoholism, concluding that the children of alcoholics could be shielded from the disease if reared away from their parents. Thirty-six children of alcoholic parents who had been taken from their families and raised in foster homes were included in her analysis. When examined in their thirties, none of them—70 percent of whom were drinkers—showed any signs of difficulty with alcohol. Her inference was that alcoholism was probably not inherited, and that its more common occurrence in children raised by alcoholic parents must be an effect of the environment in which they were raised.

Environmental circumstances that could play a role in the development of alcoholism might include the example set by an alcoholic parent; when the offspring of an alcoholic is confronted with a seemingly insurmountable problem, he or she may turn to alcohol for solace, as did the parent, even though the idea was once distasteful.

In considering alcoholism, many others see it as a form of emotional illness joined to an addiction. The alcoholic, this view holds, was emotionally troubled to begin with, before he or she started drinking. And to bolster that opinion, they list a variety of traits that seem to be characteristic of the alcoholic and problem drinker. Among these are that drinkers may be sexually and emotionally immature or deprived, strongly dependent on someone or something, troubled by feelings of inadequacy, psychoneurotic, unable to tolerate tension, guilt-ridden, easily frustrated, extremely sensitive, impulsive, hostile or convinced that they are more capable than they are. One study of multiple drug and excessive alcohol users, also conducted in Brookline, Massachusetts, by the Medical Foundation, found that users were more likely than nonusers to score poorly in studies, come from single-parent homes, have psychiatric help, be less able to talk to their parents, be less religious, feel they have more personal problems than their friends, and be more alienated from society. Sigmund Freud, whose work and theories have influenced generations of psychiatrists and psychologists, proposed that excessive drinking may represent attempts to express unconscious homosexual instincts—the heavy drinker imbibing to cover a submerged personality disorder. Freud also theorized that alcoholism stemmed from strong oral influence during childhood, that is, was related to the pleasurable early experience of sucking. Still others have linked excessive drinking to an unconscious desire to dominate or an inability to accept or give love.

"The excessive drinker," wrote Dr. David C. McClelland of Harvard in *Psychology Today* a few years ago, "is the man with an excessive need for personal power who has chosen drinking as the way to accentuate his feeling of power." As men drink, the social relations authority reported, their thoughts of power increase but, he added, there was no substantiation for the widely held psychiatric belief that drinking is accompanied by oral gratification or dependency fantasies.

"What did increase regularly with drinking were power thoughts, thoughts of having impact on others, of aggression, of sexual conquest, of being big, strong and influential," he said. It became apparent, Dr. McClelland noted, that power thoughts took two forms—S-power, or the desire to have power to help others, and P-power, the desire for power to dominate others. Dr. McClelland studied university fraternity men and found that after two or three cocktails, S-power thoughts predominate in fantasies. "A person thinks more about power, but in a relatively controlled way," he reported. "After heavier drinking, say six cocktails, fear-anxiety thoughts decrease and so do thoughts about time—being on time, worry over being late and so forth. We take this to mean that the person is becoming less reality oriented and less inhibited, but this effect appears only after fairly heavy drinking. As one becomes less inhibited, a less controlled type of power concern dominates his thinking. S-power thoughts drop out, and P-power thoughts predominate."

It has also been suggested that alcoholics are self-destructive, that those whose drinking is unbridled are literally drinking themselves to death out of guilt, punishing themselves for things that they may or may not have done. They may also be punishing those close to them for real or imagined wrongs done to the drinker—the punishment being the suffering they cause their friends and relatives.

"Although there are infinite variations on the basic theme," observes the AMA *Manual*, "psychoanalytic theory generally holds that alcoholism is the result of early emotional deprivation and disturbances, with consequent emotional immaturity. The alcoholic relies on the effects of alcohol to relieve such feelings as anxiety, hostility, inferiority or depression which are reflections of much deeper and usually unrecognized patterns of marked insecurity, rage or guilt. The use of the drug to attain relief is reinforced through repetition, and its abuse evolves as an habitual response to internal discomfort."

Some behavioral scientists see alcoholism as a learned response—the drinker discovers that his or her reward for drinking may be a calming of anxieties. So, a drinking pattern is established, and soon anxiety becomes a sort of bell—when it "rings" in the individual, the automatic response to it is to use the deadening effect of liquor. If alcoholism is part of a learned behavior pattern, theoretically it should be possible to "unlearn" it, a possibility that will be discussed in the chapter on treatment.

The trouble with attempting to draw a personality profile of an alcoholic is that while the traits that have been mentioned are often found among alcoholics, they also appear in men and women who are not alcoholic, and who may be either mentally ill or normal. The psychological theories do not tell us why people with the same life-styles and hang-ups as the alcoholic do not, for the most part, become alcoholics. Then, too, critics of the psychological approach sometimes say, a hard, firm list of the kinds of people who become addicted may not be of much value if the classification system has sprung from only people *known* to be addicted. Another difficulty is in determining whether the behavior and traits that have been collected and filed under alcoholism are causes or effects of the heavy drinking. Does one drink heavily, for instance, because of depression? Or, does the drinker become depressed because of the drinking?

When dealing with such a complicated subject as alcoholism, with its varying degrees of severity and all of the other factors and influences that affect drinking patterns—it is nearly impossible to come up with the neat pigeonholes that all of us would like to see. Says the NIAAA report:

The causative factors in alcoholism operate within a specific environment. Thus, for example, it has become increasingly clear that a familial learning factor is important in the genesis of alcoholism in certain people. However, the expression of a familial factor occurs only when the environmental circumstances permit it. This well-known phenomenon has recently been elaborated in relation to the sociology of medicine and of chronic diseases. Thus, we commonly speak of "the cause" of tuberculosis as being the tubercle bacillus. However, even knowing this, it remains to be specified why and under what circumstances some people get TB and others do not. Furthermore, it appears that tuberculosis was on the decline because of social factors, such as relief of crowding and the improvement of housing conditions, even before the cause was known. In an analogous way, we may hope substantially to improve the conditions surrounding alcohol-related behavior long before we are able to specify so-called "first causes."

Too much emphasis on discovering a cause—and, indeed, a satisfactory cause may never be found—could draw attention away from treatment, much as attempting to find the secret of longer life could make scientists neglect improving the lot of the elderly in our population. Whatever the cause of alcoholism and problem drinking, be it physiological or psychological, the afflicted individuals are all brothers and sisters stamped with the same ugly brand. They are our brothers and sisters, too.

Four

Alcohol: What It Is and How It Works

◆·◆·◆

MARTY: Beer is what I drink mostly. I love it. Getting shit-faced is very common. I seem to have a super good time when I get that way. I don't do it every night; however I do on weekends. You can pick chicks up easy when you're high. Mostly because they get shit-faced just as much. I don't mess around with drugs. Beer can get me my high, so that's all I do.

◆·◆·◆

In examining some of the reasons why people drink to excess, the statement was made that it is often difficult to determine whether the behavioral problems associated with drinking are causes or effects. A safe answer would be that both apply, but that each case must be looked at individually.

Alcohol, of course, does have an effect on body and mind. Sometimes, the effect may be predicted with a fair amount of accuracy, such as how fast it will take an individual to get drunk and on how much liquor. In other cases, as in judging which drinker will get cancer or ulcers or will become depressed enough to commit suicide, it is harder to say.

Before considering some of the serious things that can happen to drinkers that will be discussed in the next chapter, perhaps it would be helpful to understand a little about the chemical nature of this substance we are talking about, and how it works in the body.

We are dealing here only with ethyl alcohol, or ethanol, since this is the principal chemical in distilled liquor, wine and beer. It should not be confused with methyl alcohol, of methanol, which can be extremely toxic and which can cause nerve damage and blindness, even if taken in small amounts. Ethyl, or beverage alcohol, is a natural substance, colorless and inflammable, produced by the reaction of fermenting sugar with yeast spores. Aristotle and Hippocrates, among the early Greeks, knew of its mysterious presence in wine and called it "spirits." Ethanol is also widely used as a solvent, an agent which dissolves a substance, and in the preparation of other compounds.

Methanol, on the other hand, was originally produced by the distillation of wood, and is not used as a beverage. It is used, however, as an antifreeze for automobiles, as a solvent and as rocket fuel.

Ethyl alcohol may also be produced in the human intestines when dietary sugars are fermented; but in the body it is detoxified before it can do any injury by a liver enzyme called alcohol dehydrogenase. It is also found naturally in another unlikely place—outer space. Late in 1974, an international team of radio astronomers discovered ethanol floating about in a vast cloud of dust and gas while studying the constellation Sagittarius, some thirty thousand light years away. The finding was not totally unexpected because scientists have identified a number of other organic molecules in space, methyl alcohol and ammonia among them.

Beer and ale contain the lowest alcohol content, beer between 4 and 4.5 percent; ale, slightly more; and malt liquor, of the same family, around 6 percent. Beer makers may not, under the law, disclose the alcoholic strength on the labels of their products, but other beverages are so labeled. Dinner wines such as Burgundy, zinfandel and Chablis run anywhere from 10 to 14 percent alcohol, with fortified wines like sherry and port containing from 17 to 20 percent. These latter wines, often used as dessert wines (although sherry is sometimes drunk before meals if it is of a dry, or less sweet kind), are fortified by the addition of more alcohol to strengthen them. Brandy, a stronger alcoholic drink distilled from wine or from the fermented juice of fruits, is often used to fortify wines. Distilled liquor—whiskey, gin, scotch, vodka and rum—is the result of further concentration of alcohol produced by fermentation. These so-called hard liquors contain from around 40 percent to 75 percent alcohol, expressed on the bottle labels as "proof." The actual amount of alcohol in the liquor is one half the proof number. For example, 86 proof (which is what most whiskeys are) contains 43 percent alcohol; 100 proof vodka is 50 percent alcohol; the strongest liquor available in the United States, 151-proof rum, is about 75 percent alcohol.

What we drink affects us at different speeds, although it's good to remember that any alcoholic beverage drunk in large quantity will cause intoxication. Many drinkers delude themselves into thinking there are certain "safe" drinks. This is not true, and one should always have a healthy respect for any alcoholic beverage; the best advice is to be wary of what alcohol can do, just as one should always be wary of the sea and of guns. A "shot" of liquor in a cocktail, usually measured as an ounce, contains as much alcohol as does a twelve-ounce can of beer or an average serving of wine. That is, about a half ounce of pure alcohol. A "few beers," then, may not be as harmless as it sounds, particularly if they are drunk quickly. Nor should one take too lightly the oftheard expression, "I only drink wine, never touch the hard stuff." Abused, both beverages can cause trouble.

Wine, however, is usually taken with meals, which makes it "safer." Beer, which contains several ingredients that delay its action in the body, is most often consumed more slowly than liquor. It has also been demonstrated that beer does not affect one as quickly and as drastically as does liquor, and it is doubtful that beer is the menace it was made out to be by one early moralist, who warned: "Of all intoxicating drinks, it is the most animalizing. It dulls the intellectual and moral and feeds the sensual and beastly nature. Beyond all other drinks, it qualifies for deliberate and unprovoked crime. In this respect, it is much worse than distilled liquors."

Alcohol may correctly be termed a drug because it dramatically affects the central nervous system in much the same way as an anesthetic, and a poison, because like all drugs, excessive amounts can injure health or even kill. Early in 1974, in fact, at least three tragic deaths linked to excessive drinking made the news. In South Boston, a sixteen-year-old boy died after drinking a pint of vodka without pausing. He did it, apparently, on a bet with his friends. And in Fort Walton Beach, Florida, two men in their thirties died after each consumed more than a quart of gin in an hour. They had been trying to settle a long-standing argument over who would drink the most.

Alcohol is also classed as a food because it contains calories and provides energy. An ounce and a half of whiskey, for instance, contains about 125 calories—almost the same number as found in a cup of canned pineapple or an ounce of cheddar cheese. But alcohol has no nutritional worth whatsoever, and one cannot live on such a food alone, no more than one can live on candy bars and cola. Remember that next time you hear someone say that four martinis, with around 130 calories each, can supply a person living on 2,000 calories a day with a fifth to a quarter of daily caloric intake. Even adding vitamins probably would not help since heavy alcohol ingestion interferes with their proper use in the body. Furthermore, any idea that alcoholics eat poorly because of the calories they obtain from drinking is erroneous. Researchers believe that the reason alcoholics do not eat well is because they have learned that the less they eat, the more they will become intoxicated. This matter of how food affects the presence of alcohol in the system is an important one that will be examined a bit later.

While alcohol is a food, it is not digested—broken down and converted so it can be taken to cells and tissues by blood plasma, the liquid part of the blood. Almost the moment alcohol reaches the stomach it begins to bypass the normal digestive route. About 20 percent of it is absorbed directly into the bloodstream through the stomach walls, and heads straight for the brain and all the other organs and tissues of the body. The rest is processed at a slightly slower rate through the gastrointestinal tract into the bloodstream. Because it is dissolved in the water contained in the body, more alcohol shows up in organs with an ample water supply. Blood is 90 percent water, and the brain has a good blood supply, hence the effects of alcohol may be felt rather quickly. Acting on the brain's central switchboard, the alcohol slows down or depresses activity. At first, after a drink or two, there is a feeling of tranquility, of well-being, of warmth. Then, as drinking progresses, the drinker begins to talk freely as he or she loses some degree of restraint and sometimes begins to act and talk more openly than when not drinking, possibly becoming aggressive or depressed. The upper front lobes of the brain, which control judgment, are now affected. Depending on the speed at which liquor is consumed and the amount and kind of food in the stomach, the drinker's hearing may become dulled, speech slurred and vision impaired as the alcohol begins to saturate other areas of the brain. Memory is affected, and muscle control is lost. The drinker gets dizzy and may be unable to stand erect or walk a straight line. As the upper limits of saturation are reached with more drinking, unconsciousness—the expression is "dead drunk"—may occur, along with below normal temperature and, ultimately, death. This progression, from euphoria to loss of consciousness, is often difficult to chart accurately. That is to say, it's not easy to tell whether such and such will actually happen to a drinker after a given number of drinks. Alcohol affects each of us differently, and several variables must be considered.

One of these variables is the rate at which alcohol is absorbed into the blood. How fast it affects the brain and body depends on several factors, among them: the pace at which one drinks, whether or not there is food in the stomach, how much one weighs, the setting in which one is drinking and what one drinks. We have already said that beer contains substances that retard the absorption of alcohol, substances which have been removed from hard liquor during distillation. Diluting an alcoholic beverage with water also slows down the absorption, but mixing with carbonated water, so-called club soda, increases the rate of absorption due to the carbon dioxide content which bubbles the alcohol quickly on its way. For this reason, champagne and other sparkling wines affect the brain faster than other wines.

In discussing how fast one drinks, it is helpful to know how the body goes about ridding itself of the alcohol consumed. As the circulating blood transports the alcohol through the body, a disposal system is automatically turned on. About 10 percent is expelled directly from the lungs in the exhaled air, and through the kidneys into the urine; minute amounts are excreted in saliva, tears, sweat and gastric juice. The remainder is oxidized in the liver. This is a process similar to combustion or burning in which fuel is consumed to liberate energy and heat. Dissolved food in the blood is combined with oxygen to release energy, and in so doing it is broken down into carbon dioxide and water. These are returned to the blood as the waste products of oxidation. So alcohol, as a food, is oxidized and discarded, or burned up—after providing heat and energy, measured in calories, to the body. As a general rule, it takes about an hour for the half ounce of pure alcohol in an ounce of liquor, a can of beer or a glass of wine to be oxidized. This means that as long as one doesn't have more than one drink in that hour, the disposal system will work smoothly because the alcohol has not had a chance to build up in the blood. Sipping a drink slowly also will cut down the amount of alcohol that must be absorbed at once. If liquor is consumed in this manner—slowly and at the same rate the body is able to burn it off—the drinker will remain sober and suffer little, if any, unpleasant side effects. Downing one's liquor, however, in the traditional "bottoms up" fashion, or chug-a-lugging beer, will drive more alcohol into the bloodstream, jolting the nervous system and bringing on intoxication—an end that does not fit into responsible drinking behavior. Gulping, in any event, is always a gross habit, whether it be beer or steak.

The amount and kind of food one has in the stomach also slow down the absorption of alcohol by, in effect, mopping it up and diluting it in the food's water content. When liquor is drunk either after or during the meal, its effects are less potent than they would be if the alcohol is swallowed before meals. "The Frenchman having wine with his *boeuf bourguignon* or the German washing down his *wurst* with beer," observes Dr. Frederic W. Nordsiek, a nutrition expert, in the Massachusetts Institute of Technology publication, *Technology Review*, "may with impunity imbibe more alcohol than Americans who cushion their preprandial (before meals) martinis with only a few salted peanuts." Foods that are high in protein are the best brakes one can put on alcohol in a hurry to get into the bloodstream. These would include meat, fish, eggs, milk and cheese. They retard absorption partly because members of the protein family stay behind in the stomach for a longer time than other foodstuffs. It has also been shown that drinks mixed with foods or juices—milk, eggs, orange and tomato juice, for example—weaken alcohol's "kick" to varying degrees.

A person's weight is responsible for some startling differences in how alcohol acts. The general rule is that the lighter weight individual, drinking the same amount of liquor as a heavier person, is likely to feel its impact more. This is so because heavier individuals have more water in their systems with which to dilute alcohol. Because alcohol is distributed quickly and uniformly within the circulatory system, the heavier person gets a smaller concentration in the bloodstream.

Your frame of mind and the circumstances under which you consume liquor also determine how fast alcohol affects you. If you are comfortably seated and relaxed, drinking with a friend, alcohol will not have as much effect as when you are standing and drinking, as at a cocktail party. If you are emotionally upset and tired, the alcohol also may have a strong effect on your mind and body. In addition, what you expect from your drinking is important. That is, if you believe drunkenness is going to result, it really will come on more easily.

What makes us feel alcohol in our brain is the level of alcohol in the blood, and this level and the degree of intoxication can be measured. Blood, urine and breath can be tested. One of the common methods is with the drunkometer (also called a breathometer or intoximeter), a device that allows the rapid measurement of alcohol in the air breathed out by a person suspected of being drunk.

While individual differences do exist, it is generally accepted that when a person has a concentration of five-hundredths of one percent (0.05 percent) or less of alcohol in the bloodstream, he or she is sober. At 0.05 percent, inhibitions may be lessened and judgment adversely affected, and it is at or around this stage that the drinker usually experiences the feelings of warmth, relaxation and well-being. Depending on the amount of liquor and the other variables cited earlier, this state might be achieved after two or three cocktails or two or three large cans of beer. (When liquor is added to a cocktail mix, it is measured in "shot" glasses or "jiggers." A "shot" is an ounce, a "jigger" an ounce and a half. Some measuring glasses contain two ounces. Three cocktails made with one-ounce measures equal two made with the larger "jigger." Using the two-ounce measure is the wrong way to begin an evening's drinking. It is, therefore, not enough to assess one's total consumption merely by talking in terms of so many drinks or cans of beer or glasses of wine because of the differences in measure.)

A person with 0.05 percent level of alcohol in his blood is considered legally sober—a fact that does not mean, however, that the drinker is really as sober as the person who hasn't had anything to drink. Numerous studies have shown that even at that level a person's ability to drive an automobile or operate machinery may be impaired. One survey by the National Transportation Safety Board found that the chances of a driver causing a highway accident increased at .04 percent, was four times as great at .06 percent and six times as great at .08 percent. Some states have set .08 percent as the measure for legal drunkenness, others make it .15 percent, which is what the National Safety Council has adopted regarding the operation of a motor vehicle. You should know that the blood-alcohol level is not a true picture of one's ability to drive. "In fact," says the American Automobile Association,

the potential car operator may be much further down the road to intoxication and impairment than even a breathalyzer, blood or urine test may indicate. Today's safety specialists are placing a lot of emphasis on the blood-alcohol percentage level, even to the point of furnishing charts indicating how many ounces of alcohol a person may drink before becoming intoxicated, In theory, this would be fine if a driver could check a chart and say to himself, "I'm only going to have X number of drinks, according to my physical size, then I'll quit and still be able to drive safely." Unfortunately it doesn't work that way.

The AAA goes on to cite the other factors that enter the picture: how tired the potential driver is, the amount and kind of food eaten, whether medications have been taken, what kind of day it's been at home, school or work. In addition, even under similar conditions the same amount of alcohol may have a completely different effect the very next time the driver drinks.

Most people are definitely intoxicated at levels of 0.15 percent, after consuming six or seven cocktails in a short period of time. They are unable to walk normally and control their emotions. At this stage, it may take as long as ten hours for the alcohol to leave the system. (Usually, it requires about as many hours as the number of drinks to sober up completely. Intoxication disappears as the alcohol is metabolized.)

At 0.25 percent, reached after drinking about twelve ounces of whiskey in a few hours, vomiting and lack of comprehension may result. At .30 percent, the drinker may be described as "stuporous," totally confused, and at .40 percent becomes unconscious. Death can occur between 0.40 percent and 0.70 percent, but this, thankfully, is a rare event because usually unconsciousness puts a stop to further drinking. Nevertheless, downing sixteen ounces of liquor, one pint, can kill instantly and is a practice obviously not recommended.

We have said that beer does not affect one as quickly or as dramatically as liquor; that is, when the alcoholic content of the two beverages is identical. In the *Technology Review* article mentioned earlier, Dr. Nordsiek calls attention to a study done some years ago by Dr. Leonard Goldberg of Sweden's Karolinska Institute. "A large body of data," Dr. Goldberg is quoted as saying, "has made it clear that different alcoholic beverages, containing equal quantities of absolute alcohol, do not produce identical blood alcohol levels when ingested. Distilled spirits give the highest levels, fortified wines somewhat lower ones, light wines still lower and beers the lowest." To demonstrate this, Dr. Goldberg had moderate drinkers swallow either beer or liquor over a half-hour period. One group drank five one-ounce shots of whiskey, the other five twelve-ounce servings of beer. Blood samples were taken every half hour, until the alcohol had disappeared completely from the drinkers' blood some seven hours later. Commented Dr. Nordsiek: "The whiskey sent blood alcohol soaring to a peak within one hour; whereas the beer had its maximum effect only after about two hours. And even then, the highest blood alcohol produced by the beer was barely half as great as that produced by the whiskey. Finally, alcohol disappeared from the blood of the beer drinkers substantially sooner. Noteworthy is that, according to drunken driving laws, the whiskey drinkers became drunk whereas the beer drinkers did not."

You might ask if it's possible to purge alcohol from the system faster than the built-in oxidation mechanism can; that is, bring on the sober state quickly. At the present time, there is no way to do this, either with medication, a cold shower or black coffee. Once alcohol gets into the blood, there is nothing to do but wait it out. Its effects, however, can be controlled, as we have attempted to show here, if alcohol is used properly to begin with. Improperly used, it not only brings on temporary intoxication—which can contribute to problem drinking when it is viewed as "funny" and condoned—and the sickly morning-after feeling, but it can also contribute to many serious, longstanding physical and behavioral problems. We'll examine some of these next.

Five

Effects

———◆◆◆———

AL: Comparing pot to alcohol, I'd say alcohol anytime. I've tried both. On dope, you're not you, you're not even in your body. Alcohol keeps you spaced for a while, but in your own body.

———◆◆◆———

If I had a choice," Dr. Herbert Kleber, assistant professor of psychiatry at Yale University once remarked, "I would rather be a heroin addict for ten years than an alcohol addict for ten years. If I were a heroin addict, I would have done far less harm to my body and my mind than if I were an alcoholic."

The statement might seem a bit strong to some, particularly parents who are so guilty about their own drinking habits—or who are unaware that they are bad habits— that they defend themselves by saying things like, "Well, at least I never took dope." The message they're trying to convey is that their drinking behavior is the far lesser of two evils.

It is not, of course, and in the long run it may, indeed, be a lot worse. The problems the alcohol abusers can cause to themselves and to those who know them are no less severe than those afflicting the people who use other drugs as freely. The point is, alcohol is legal, relatively inexpensive, easily procured and well advertised. Heroin and cocaine may be procured with relative ease in some places, but they are none of the other things.

It's not my purpose here to point to the similarities and differences between alcoholics and drug addicts, nor to engage in a fly-casting contest to determine who can get farther from shore and with what. Suffice it to say that both alcohol and drugs are toxic to body and mind when used improperly, excessively and over a prolonged period of time.

It was noted in the last chapter that the intensity of alcohol's immediate effects on the system depends, among other things, on the amount consumed. Quantity is also important when considering the long-term physical and behavioral disorders associated with alcohol. You should bear in mind, though, that even one drink might be enough to touch off a medical problem, like an ulcer, that has been lying undiscovered in an individual. A single drink might also be all it takes to impair judgment just enough to cause death or crippling injury in an automobile or in a home workshop. Also, there are some people who simply cannot tolerate alcohol in any form or quantity. It may be said, however, with comfortable certainty, that moderate amounts of alcohol—though the substance is classified as a poison—will not harm the nonalcoholic; in other words, most people.

Unabused, alcohol does not kill our brain cells, or destroy our livers, hearts and kidneys, nor cause us to bear or father mentally-deranged or physically-deformed offspring. Furthermore, the nonexcessive use of alcohol does not appear to affect the overall mortality rate nor does it affect the mortality from the largest specific major cause of death, coronary heart disease. Indeed, there is even some preliminary evidence that the death rate of drinkers from heart disease is lower than that of abstainers and ex-drinkers. Even some diabetics, long urged to avoid alcohol completely, can drink moderately without ill effects.

Sustained, heavy use of alcohol, however, is another matter, and it is this kind of intake that is generally associated with an increased mortality rate and a host of medical complications. But again, the cautionary word about terms like "heavy," "excessive," "light" and "moderate." By themselves they mean little, and they must be used carefully. Also, some of the disorders that have appeared in so-called heavy drinkers—such as "beer-drinkers' heart," "wine-drinkers' stomach," "alcoholic pellagra" and Korsakoff's psychosis—all appear to be the result of nutritional deficiencies and not of the alcohol. Alcoholics tend to drink their meals instead of eating them, but the calories, as we said earlier, are empty, that is, without such things as proteins and vitamins that are essential to good nutrition. Hence, the tendency to develop a broad range of diseases caused by inadequate diet.

Against that background, let's first examine some of the medical problems that are or may be produced by the regular consumption of large amounts of liquor.

To begin with, consider the case of eighteen-year-old Albert J., as reported by Dr. Norman E. Zinberg, a Harvard psychiatrist, in an article in a recent issue of the *Boston Globe*. Albert had vomited a dark substance (which later turned out to be blood) and was taken to the hospital where a doctor learned that Albert had been drinking beer and wine since he was thirteen, and hard liquor for the past two years. Over the past year or so, his alcohol intake had increased sharply to the point of drinking a fifth of wine, or a couple of six-packs of beer or a pint of whiskey a day. His schoolwork had fallen off, and he had been experiencing a sour taste in his mouth, a sharp, burning sensation in his stomach and occasional vomiting. Albert connected these problems to his drinking, Dr. Zinberg reported, but told himself that everything would be fine as he got used to drinking. "The doctor was distressed particularly by Albert's total commitment to drinking, which caused the young man to overlook such serious symptoms," Dr. Zinberg wrote. "However, when he told Albert of his concern, the patient dismissed it and assured the doctor, 'I'm man enough to handle it. I can drink any of them under the table.' "

Albert's problem, aside from the fact that he was on the road to becoming an alcoholic, was gastritis, an inflammation of the lining of the stomach which, in its chronic form, arises from excess acidity, and often follows periods of heavy drinking. Erosion of the stomach lining and sometimes severe bleeding occur with the condition, usually after binge drinking. Moderate amounts of alcohol do not appear to irritate stomach tissues in those free of stomach disorders. But in ulcer sufferers, even small amounts of alcohol may stimulate enough gastric acid to further inflame the ulcer, a condition that, incidentally, seems to occur more frequently among problem drinkers. Persons with ulcers should, of course, be careful of alcoholic beverages, something not easy to do if the individuals have a drinking problem. A situation like that gives rise to another definition of an alcoholic, this one by Dr. Jay B. Shumaker, a gastroenterologist—a physician who specializes in diseases of the stomach—at the Newton-Wellesley Hospital in Massachusetts. Dr. Shumaker sees the alcoholic as someone who has a medical reason for not drinking and still does.

According to recent research, when alcohol enters the intestines from the stomach, it stimulates the production of certain fatty substances that eventually find their way into the bloodstream; this may lead to the fatty liver found in those suffering from alcoholism. The fatty substances also lead to an increase of the fatty alcohol, cholesterol, in the bloodstream; cholesterol has been implicated in a disorder called atherosclerosis, or hardening of the arteries, when excessive amounts are deposited in the arteries.

But it is the liver, the body's largest glandular organ, that plays the key role in the metabolism and detoxification of alcohol, and is the target of a number of serious chronic disorders seen in alcoholism. Located in the upper right side of the abdominal cavity, the liver is a complex chemical factory responsible for scores of bodily functions.

Among other things, it produces bile to help digest fatty foods, stores and releases sugar, manufactures heparin, an acid that keeps blood from clotting, produces antibodies to fight against disease and removes poisons; it produces enzymes, those biochemical workhorses that speed up the thousands of changes that take place continually in our bodies. Without enzymes, food would go undigested, blood cells would not be replaced and tissue would not be built. Enzymes do specific jobs, and the one that starts the breakdown of alcohol—it is called alcohol dehydrogenase, or ADH—is mainly found in the liver. Because of this, when alcohol gets in the system it puts a strain on the liver, which must call up the necessary enzyme to process it. An interesting sidelight about the metabolism of alcohol in the liver may be found in the NIAAA report:

Alcohol has commonly been thought of as a totally "foreign substance" in man. Therefore the normal function of ADH in the livers of most mammalian species—the reason for its presence—was unknown. Recent work has made it clear, however, that alcohol is normally present in all mammals, and is continually produced in the intestinal tract by the action of microorganisms on soluble sugars. Judging from the rate of production of alcohol in the intestinal contents of the rat, it may be calculated that even a total abstainer would produce enough alcohol to equal that in about a quart of 3.2 percent beer per day. The alcohol produced in the gut, however, does not reach man's brain, since ADH in the liver metabolizes almost 99 percent of it before it might move out into the general circulation. Only at the higher concentrations of alcohol introduced into the circulating blood by drinking alcohol in beverages is the ability of ADH to metabolize it temporally overwhelmed. Alcohol therefore passes from the portal (veins leading from the intestines into the liver) into the systemic circulation and is thus distributed throughout the body. It can then act upon the other organs, including the brain, producing its well-known effects on brain function.

One of the most devastating of the liver disorders affecting alcoholics is cirrhosis, in which the liver cells are replaced by scar tissue. Blood circulation is impaired and other serious complications result. Cirrhosis occurs, according to some estimates, about eight times as often among alcoholics as among nonalcoholics, and takes the lives of more than twenty thousand Americans every year. The disease also occurs in nondrinkers and can be caused not only by heavy alcohol use but by congestive heart failure, viruses, syphilis, overexposure to certain toxic chemicals, excessive consumption of sugar and soft drinks, and protein and vitamin deficiency.

There still remains a considerable difference of opinion over what role diet plays in the development of cirrhosis. Some scientists believe that a well-balanced diet protects against the disease, others feel that heavy quantities of alcohol will damage the liver even if the person is well fed. Studies have, in fact, turned up evidence to support both views. (Recent investigations also indicate that even a few weeks of daily moderate drinking can make a liver fatty and less efficient. The problem, however, can be reversed at least in the beginning stages by abstaining.)

In a ten-year experimental survey conducted in 1973, the investigators reported that it is alcohol toxicity and not nutrition that damages the liver. Their findings, based on work with rats, baboons and human volunteers, indicate that heavy amounts of alcohol do have a poisonous effect on the liver and play a major part in producing fatty liver and the hardening of tissues that precedes alcoholic cirrhosis. An earlier study found that the cirrhotic livers of a group of men who combined heavy drinking with a high-protein diet steadily improved, while the livers of those who drank and ate a low-protein diet did not improve, and in some cases worsened. A letter to the *Journal of the American Medical Association* in 1974 about the effect of alcohol on twenty-six baboons, thirteen of which were fed the equivalent of a fifth of liquor a day for up to four years, points up some of the pitfalls of laboratory experiments:

"[The investigators] reported that a fifth of liquor daily, after four years' time, produced cirrhosis in two baboons out of 13," wrote Dr. Salvatore P. Lucia of the University of California School of Medicine at San Francisco. "This is certainly not a clear indication that alcohol is toxic to the liver per se. A brutal overdose of any nutritive substance over an extended period of time will eventually produce signs or symptoms of bodily harm—be it alcohol, sugar, carrot juice or milk. Witness the force-feeding of geese for the purpose of making *pâté de foie gras!* Common sense, it is hoped, will always remain an integral part of modern scientific investigation."

If the association between alcohol, diet and cirrhosis is still somewhat murky, the connection between cirrhosis and liver cancer is not. On a worldwide basis, 60 to 90 percent of all liver cell cancer arises in cirrhotic livers. Heavy drinking also has been linked to cancer in other parts of the body—the pancreas, mouth, esophagus (food pipe), throat and larynx (voice box). Just how malignancies are touched off is not yet known. It could be the repeated contact of tissues with alcohol itself, or the result of alcohol combined, in the case of throat cancer, with tobacco smoking.

Cigarettes and alcohol are the ham and eggs of the social circuit, although the latter combination is, naturally, far more beneficial than "butts and booze." It is true, though, that one rarely if ever finds an absence of smoking in a drinking setting. In fact, people who drink heavily also smoke heavily (one study showed that more than 90 percent of men and women alcoholics were smokers), and when the two are combined, according to some researchers, the risk of developing cancer of the mouth and throat rises to fifteen times greater than the risk among those who do neither. It has also been suggested that the heavy drinker runs the same heightened risk of contracting mouth and throat cancer as the nondrinking smoker who consumes two packs or more of cigarettes a day. Here, too, there is some disagreement, with many investigators of the belief that it is smoking that is the prime culprit and not alcohol. Dr. Irving J. Selikoff, professor of medicine at Mount Sinai School of Medicine and a leading environmental cancer investigator, is quoted in a recent (1974) issue of *Medical Tribune* as saying:

"Heavy drinkers tend to be heavy smokers, but it's hard to collect data about people who drink heavily and do not smoke. There are very real statistical problems here. Since smoking by itself will produce a significant increase in cancer incidence, how does one assess the effect of drinking?" He added that there are thus far only two areas where acceptable data for combined effects have been established:

"We know that asbestos exposure sharply increases the

lung cancer risk in smokers. The data also indicate that this is true of uranium miners who smoke."

Dr. Selikoff emphasized that more data need to be gathered and that some way must be found to separate the effect of drinking from the effect of cigarette smoking. Only then can a definite conclusion be drawn about the role of alcohol in mouth cancer.

The question of what happens when two drugs, nicotine and alcohol, enter the body simultaneously has also been explored. Dr. Henry Murphree of the Rutgers University Center for Alcohol Studies has done some careful research along this line. Working with sixteen subjects, he provided each with enough vodka and orange juice to raise the blood alcohol content to about 0.07 percent. (You'll recall that a person with 0.15 percent blood alcohol may be considered legally drunk; a person with 0.10 percent is legally impaired.)

Dr. Murphree then tested them to see how well they were able to concentrate and to duplicate geometrical figures or symbols. He also wanted to find out how they reacted to conditions including: not smoking, smoking cigarettes with low nicotine content, and smoking cigarettes with a high nicotine content.

The first thing the subjects had to do was duplicate the geometric symbols fifteen seconds after seeing them. Next, they had to try to keep a pointer on a spot on a slowly moving turntable, and to do it for two minutes. Each person had three tries at following the spot.

There was a significant decrease in ability to perform tests when shifting from a low-nicotine to a high-nicotine cigarette. The shift from a high-nicotine cigarette to no smoking produced a gain in test performance. The reverse, shifting from no smoking to a high-nicotine cigarette, tended to confirm the previous finding, because test performance was markedly and adversely affected.

Before beginning the study, Dr. Murphree had assumed that he would find that nicotine improved the performance of an intoxicated person. But the results of his test did not confirm this. Instead, nicotine accentuated the harmful effect of alcohol on coordination.

Another interesting finding from the study was the persistence of the effect of a high-nicotine cigarette in the body. After smoking one of them, several subjects were tested immediately and again after a half-hour rest period.

The half hour was not long enough to allow the nicotine effect to dissipate. Test performance continued to be adversely affected, despite the rest period.

Whether or not alcohol damages the heart and circulation is also a matter of dispute. It is known that moderate amounts slightly increase the heart rate and dilate (enlarge or stretch) blood vessels in arms, legs and skin. Blood pressure may rise, but it usually drops as the sedative effect of the alcohol sets in. With regard to more serious effects, recent studies suggest that alcohol, more often in heavy amounts, injures the myocardium, the thick muscular wall of the heart. The resulting condition is called alcoholic cardiomyopathy. For years, many physicians questioned whether there really was such a condition, but today alcoholic heart disease, the layperson's term for cardiomyopathy, is generally recognized as such. Experiments on animals and humans have demonstrated that alcohol does, in fact, harm the heart muscle. At Tulane University a few years ago, Dr. George E. Burch fed pure alcohol to mice and produced such damage, thus strongly suggesting that alcohol has a direct effect on the heart. And in a study at Boston's Lemuel Shattuck Hospital in 1972, Dr. David H. Spodick of Tufts Medical School found that heart action was less efficient due to damage to the myocardium in twenty-six alcoholics who had been consuming up to a quart of liquor daily. The patients, who had no clinical signs of heart trouble before the tests, were discovered to have heartbeats faster than normal, and other abnormalities, to indicate their hearts were not working as well as they should. It is not known, exactly, how alcohol affects the heart muscle. Some feel there is a direct, toxic effect, as suggested by the Tulane studies. Others feel that alcohol triggers a virus that does the damage, or that it upsets nutrition which in turn injures the muscle.

Insofar as coronary heart disease, or heart attack, is concerned, the evidence is not as strong, and it seems safe to say that moderate drinking does not appear to lead to this type of heart problem, the nation's number one killer. In fact, some recent studies indicate that moderate alcohol use may even be tied to lower risk of heart attack. This somewhat unusual finding has caused some scientists to wonder whether alcohol might actually be a protector of sorts. One such report, presented to the 1973 meeting of the American Heart Association by a group from the

Kaiser-Permanente Medical Care Program, dealt with a study of 464 persons who had suffered a first heart attack, each of whom had a checkup at some time prior to the attack. At checkup time, each person filled out a questionnaire which included questions about usage of tobacco, coffee, aspirin and alcohol. The answers were compared to those of persons who also completed the checkup questionnaire, but who did not later suffer heart attacks. When the results were tallied, it was discovered that there were more teetotalers among those who later suffered a heart attack than among the control groups. (The control group did not suffer heart attacks.) Also, in the group which suffered heart attacks later, fewer reported that they drank over three or over six drinks per day. The researchers who presented the report said that the explanation for the apparent slightly decreased risk of heart attack among users of alcohol in the study was not clear. Furthermore, they cautioned that their results "do not yet warrant the conclusions that drinking alcohol has a protective effect."

Another heart study, done in Los Angeles, also indicated that alcohol was not a risk factor for heart attack. The data gathered not only suggested that drinkers have a lower heart attack rate, but that persons who cut down or quit their drinking over the twelve years of the study had higher rates of coronary disease. One explanation offered for the last finding was that people in poorer health are more prone to heart disease, and on advice of their physicians are also more apt to decrease or stop their drinking.

While it has not been firmly proven that alcohol has a protective quality about it with regard to the heart—particularly among persons who have other high-risk earmarks—one can be reasonably certain, given the evidence to date, that when alcohol is drunk in moderation it will not lead to heart attacks in most people. This should not be taken to mean, of course, that all ex-drinkers or every heart disease patient should return to drinking. Such a move could, in many instances, prove to be not only injurious to health but fatal. In fact, a recent report in the *Journal of the American Medical Association* by Dr. Lawrence D. Horwitz of the University of Texas Health Science Center warned that patients with heart disease can have a marked slowing in heart action from just one drink of two ounces of whiskey. Those with severe heart damage and chronic heart failure should probably not drink at all,

Dr. Horwitz suggested. Other heart patients, he added, should be limited to a maximum daily drink of one shot of one and a half ounces of whiskey, or one twelve-ounce can of beer, or a six-ounce glass of wine. Further, Dr. Horwitz warned that patients with coronary heart disease should refrain for two hours after drinking from activity that could induce angina.

There are many other physiological complications associated with the abuse of alcohol. Among these is a little understood disorder called hemochromatosis, whose sufferers often have abnormal amounts of iron in their blood, liver disease, diabetes and dark skin. It was generally thought to be due to genetic inheritance because its signs were occasionally found in two or more members of the same family. Some years ago, however, scientists at Boston City Hospital's Mallory Institute of Pathology suggested that hemochromatosis might be a preventable environmental or dietary disease. They suggested further that it may not be a single disease entity, but one type of cirrhosis in which two conditions occur together in the same person —one in which excess iron is eaten or drunk, and a second in which there is liver disease, usually due to alcoholism or malnutrition. Drs. Richard A. MacDonald and Giselle S. Pechet told the 1964 meeting of the American Association of Pathology and Bacteriology that the disease seemed to be unusually common in some patients seen at Boston Hospital—patients who were heavy and chronic users of wine. (Wine has been found to contain large amounts of iron, but this is not believed to be harmful, and the cirrhosis of the liver that develops is similar to that which occurs when excess alcohol of any type is consumed without an adequate diet.) As an interesting sidelight, the doctors noted that in some countries—as in South Africa among the Bantu natives—preparation in iron pots of foods or alcoholic beverages such as "Kaffir beer" for periods of up to five days may result in chronic ingestion of unusual amounts of iron. The doctors emphasized that the iron and other metals that may be found in wine are actually beneficial for most people, provided it is not used in excess. The metals are necessary for the normal formation of blood and of many enzymes, and wine may be a palatable source of iron.

Another medical complication of prolonged excessive drinking is sterility and an impairment of male sexual function. Physical changes do occur in the sexual organs after prolonged heavy drinking and, as Harvard's Dr. Zinberg has pointed out, many chronic male alcoholics look feminine. He adds, however, that such changes are also found in patients with severe liver disease who are not alcoholics, which leads to the assumption that the relationship between alcohol and liver disease is at the crux of feminization among alcoholics. However, he says, careful study in recent years has turned up male alcoholics who were feminized before liver disease set in. This has led some scientists to conclude that alcohol itself may cause feminization by weakening the role of the male hormones —just as liver disease brings on feminine characteristics by upsetting the normal liver-controlled hormone balance.

Looking at the effects of high alcohol intake on another level—that of the cell, the basic unit of life—there is evidence linking alcoholism to a complication called thrombocytopenia. This is a disorder in which there is an abnormally small number of blood platelets in the circulating blood. (Platelets, also called thrombocytes, are small, colorless, disc-shaped particles that help the blood to clot.) Alcohol also appears to have something to do with bone marrow abnormalities (blood cells are formed in this soft tissue) and with the body's failure to manufacture red blood cells in some disorders. Harvard Medical School researchers have found, for example, that the excessive and prolonged use of alcohol can inhibit the normal development of red cells by blocking the growth-promoting action of folic acid, a necessary ingredient in the body. "If alcohol intake is unchecked over a lengthy period of time," Dr. Louis W. Sullivan told an annual meeting of the American Society for Clinical Nutrition, "one form of anemia, in which red blood cells are imperfectly formed, results." Dr. Sullivan found also that some 45 percent of the chronic alcoholic patients seen at Boston City Hospital have folic acid deficiency.

In the brain, also, where alcohol is carried by the blood, cells are affected. The brain, we all know, is the single organ vital to behavior, both violent and peaceful. An intricate computer, it is strongly influenced by our environment, and by such things as lack of blood supply, pollutants and drugs, including alcohol. Some researchers believe that brain cells are actually destroyed by the effects of heavy alcohol use, others that the cells are merely temporarily

75

changed; still others feel that any brain cell changes that do show up after repetitive heavy use of liquor are caused by poor nutrition, not by the alcohol. There is, at any rate, little evidence that *moderate* amounts of alcohol have any appreciable effect on the permanent structure or function of the brain or any other nerve tissues.

Studies at Downstate Medical Center in Brooklyn have shown that feeding large amounts of alcohol to mice produces changes in a brain chemical known as NAD. This chemical is important to the transmission of nerve impulses. And, some years ago at the Worcester Foundation for Experimental Biology in Massachusetts, scientists turned up evidence that metabolites (the product of metabolism) of a hormonelike substance, serotonin, may play a part in evoking the effects of alcohol upon behavior.

An interesting discussion of how alcohol causes brain cell changes appeared a few years ago in the magazine *Today's Health*, published by the American Medical Association. Dr. Marvin A. Block, former chairman of the AMA's Committee on Alcoholism, noted that after prolonged dousing with alcohol, the chemistry of brain cells is so altered that alcohol becomes a necessity for cell function. In other words, the heavy drinker who starts out looking for bottled courage or escape may wind up needing alcohol for the brain cells just as a diabetic needs insulin injections for the sugar-using cells of his or her body.

"We do know that the protoplasm of the cells—particularly the brain cells—is affected by chemicals introduced, whether alcohol, barbiturates or other drugs," said Dr. Block. And, if the use of such drugs continues, the cells soon develop a tolerance for the drug. After tolerance is established, Dr. Block said, the cell proceeds to develop a necessity for having the drug present in order to function. "We now have physiological or physical dependence," he explained.

When alcohol, narcotics or other addictive drugs upon which the cells have become dependent are suddenly withdrawn, the cells must reorganize their way of life, much as they did in becoming addicted. The strain, however, is more intense.

"The cell may undergo something comparable to a convulsion in order to accommodate itself to functioning without the drug upon which it became dependent," Dr. Block said. This withdrawal reaction of the cells is in turn passed on to the individual, where it is manifest as convulsions, delirium tremens, hallucinations, or the shakes if the reaction is mild. Addiction at the cellular level, Dr. Block added, has been documented in the laboratory with both narcotics and alcohol.

He pointed out that doctors at the University of Michigan Medical School, for example, have shown that live human cells outside the body can become addicted to morphine when the drug is added to their environment. Some of the cells die when morphine is suddenly withdrawn from their diet after they have become addicted.

Also, researchers at Georgetown University, according to Dr. Block, have reported a convulsion of alcohol-addicted cells when alcohol is withdrawn. The wall of the cell apparently undergoes the convulsion.

The ability of cells to become addicted, Dr. Block said, helps explain why a person can never truly be cured of alcoholism. "A cure would imply that the individual could go back to normal drinking," he observed. "But this is not true. Once the alcoholic addiction, with physiologic dependence, is established, reintroduction of alcohol into the person's cells will immediately start the craving again. This has been proved by millions of alcoholics who have tried to go back to normal drinking and have failed."

Excessive drinking habits can also affect human beings in another way. If, for instance, a woman drinks heavily during pregnancy, the alcohol that intoxicates her is passed along to the fetus nestled in her body. The fetus not only becomes intoxicated also, but will most likely suffer withdrawal symptoms at birth. Worse, there is the real danger that the child will be born seriously deformed. At a conference on genetics and birth defects held in Boston in 1973 under the auspices of the National Foundation—March of Dimes, Dr. Kenneth L. Jones of the University of Washington School of Medicine revealed that he and his group had studied eight unrelated children, all of whose mothers were chronic alcoholics during pregnancy; the children had a pattern of face, head, limb and cardiovascular defects. The head defects included microcephaly, an abnormally small head resulting from premature hardening of the skull and closure of the openings. Limb defects included abnormalities of joints and altered palm crease patterns. Heart defects were primarily septal problems that involve the muscular walls dividing the chambers.

"To our knowledge," Dr. Jones told the meeting, "this is the first reported association between maternal alcoholism and a unique pattern of malformation in the offspring."

All of the children, he added, were small for their age and remained low in height and weight averages. Their average IQ was 63 points, compared to a normal score of 100, and ranged from below 50 to the middle 70s.

Studies are continuing in a number of medical centers on other facets of the mother's alcoholism that might affect the fetus, such as cirrhosis and nutritional deficiencies.

Alcohol, as everyone knows, also can alter the way we act, for better or for worse, and it is a factor in how long we live. Let's look first at how it affects behavior.

There's ample proof that liquor stimulates aggressive behavior, both in humans and in animals. In fact, one does not need to look far for the person, male or female, who is ready for a verbal or a fist fight after a few drinks. This aggression has been graphically demonstrated in the laboratory with Siamese Fighting Fish (*Betta splendens*) which have been bred for centuries and have developed brilliant coloring, long fins and extreme pugnacity. When alcohol is added to their tankwater, their fighting behavior becomes more vicious. Rats, too, become more belligerent while under the influence. At Boston City Hospital and at McLean Hospital in Belmont, Massachusetts, neurobiologist David Ingle and his colleagues recently poured the equivalent of two dozen martinis into a tank containing goldfish, and after the fish were, in Dr. Ingle's words, "good and drunk," a number of tests were administered. "With a little alcohol, they learn faster and better," said Dr. Ingle. "With a bigger dose, they get depressed and don't learn very well. They don't even pay attention. If they get moderately drunk, like humans at a party, they suffer loss of memory, become aggressive, or lose all fear and judgment."

Controlled experiments with people have turned up similar behavior patterns. In one measurement of aggressive behavior, the subjects were asked to administer electric shocks of varying intensity to their colleagues. The people doing the shocking were divided into two groups: one group was allowed to drink alcohol, the other was not. The result was that those who had drunk liquor administered stronger shocks. In another experiment, volunteers were divided into groups and invited to "parties" in which liquor or soft drinks were served, and several competitive indoor games played. There was more aggressive game-playing and other behavior among those at the "wet" party than at the "dry," with hard liquor drinkers more belligerent than the beer drinkers. Other studies have confirmed that people who drink beverages with higher congener counts such as whiskeys are apt to take more risks than those who drink gin or vodka. (Congeners—substances such as fusel oil, tannin, aldehydes and acetic acid—appear in all alcoholic beverages in varying amounts. They are by-products of the fermentation process, or they are drawn from wooden containers used in aging some beverages. They are why a certain drink is a whiskey or a vodka or a wine, since they give alcoholic beverages their characteristic odor, color and taste. In general, the higher the congener count, the heavier the taste and odor and the darker the color. Little is known about how the congeners affect the human body, but recent research has blamed them for a number of adverse psychological effects.) In the goldfish study mentioned earlier, it was found that the fish stayed drunk longer on bourbon than on straight alcohol.

Alcohol has also been connected to the commission of rape. Richard T. Rada of the University of New Mexico told a meeting of the American Psychiatric Association recently that alcoholism is significantly related to such assault. Of seventy-seven rapists at a treatment center, 35 percent were found to be alcoholics and half were drinking at the time of the rape. The researchers suggested that therapy for rapists should concentrate on alcoholic as well as sexual problems.

It should be noted again here that alcohol has different effects on different people. Not everyone who drinks, of course, is going to become violent, rape or kill. The amount of liquor consumed, the surroundings in which it is drunk and the frame of mind of the drinker are important. A study at the Massachusetts General Hospital, for instance, found an increase rather than a decrease in feelings of anxiety among alcoholics as drinking progressed. Most students of alcoholism, the report on the study said, accept as self-evident the notion that alcohol neutralizes anxiety or in some way increases the effectiveness of defense mechanisms against anxiety. "While it may be that drinking eases aberrant behavior drives, softens the pangs of conscience or lessens depression in non-alcoholics," said

Dr. Jack H. Mendelson, a psychiatrist at the MGH, "there has been no direct evidence that the same effects obtain in alcoholics."

Studies in other medical centers have also shown that alcoholics become not only more anxious after drinking but more depressed and hostile, and that their drinking, instead of heightening their feelings of self-esteem, actually makes them feel guiltier and more worthless. The depression may lead to suicide attempts, something not uncommon among alcoholics. In one study at Duke University Medical Center, twenty-six of twenty-nine persons were intoxicated at the time of their suicide attempts, and of three who were not, two made attempts after eighteen months of being sober and while suffering depressive disorders. Eleven of the twenty-six, it also turned out, were categorized as "depressive." They experienced increasing depression, little physical activity, feelings of self-worthlessness and withdrawal from society, along with a prolonged period of continuous intoxication. Their attempts at suicide, the study found, were made quietly, while they were alone, and with apparent care and deliberation. "Whatever its causes, the depressive syndrome of chronic intoxication seems to be of especial clinical importance," Drs. Dan Montgomery and Demmie G. Mayfield reported at the Fifth World Congress of Psychiatry in 1971. "This type of alcohol-related suicide attempt appears to be highly lethal, and we would wonder if this were not the basis of a substantial number of successful attempts among alcoholics." Seven of the twenty-six showed what is known as abreactive behavior—that is, the sudden release of repressed emotions. These patients had abrupt intoxication in common (as opposed to many days or several weeks of drunkenness), as well as hyperactivity and aggressiveness. Their eruptive suicide attempts, the researchers found, were part of a hostile interpersonal relationship, such as an argument with a wife. Abreactive behavior has been identified in almost every detailed study of suicide in intoxicated subjects. Those reflecting this sort of behavior are less likely to seriously injure themselves, and in fact only seven in the study inflicted a potentially fatal wound. The "depressive syndrome," however, is another matter, and the doctors believe that its significance in suicide attempts has not been fully appreciated.

Let's turn now to how alcohol affects how long we live.

A successful suicide while a person is under the influence of liquor can, of course, be interpreted as a life-shortening effect of alcohol, just as can murders committed under the influence, or fatal accidents at home and on the highway, if too much has been drunk. "Alcohol consumption has been cited as a major factor in automobile crashes, drownings, fires, poisonings and plane crashes," observes Dr. Richard E. Boyatzis in the *Quarterly Journal of Studies on Alcohol* (September, 1974). "Although equipment malfunctions and situational factors probably account for some of these, it is likely that 'human recklessness' plays a major role. Human recklessness may be considered another label for the type of 'high risk' assertive behavior often demonstrated by persons who have been drinking."

As stated, alcohol abuse has been implicated in some ten thousand accidental deaths at home and at work every year. In one study of the relationship between alcohol consumption and nonfatal home accidents, from 1966 to 1967, a third of all patients over sixteen admitted for emergency treatment at the Massachusetts General Hospital were interviewed. There were eight thousand in all, and the presence of alcohol was determined by breath analysis. Nearly one out of four (22 percent) of the patients with injuries due to home accidents had positive readings, indicating the presence of alcohol. And among all those injured in accidents, the largest percentage of positive readings (30 percent) was found in the group injured in transportation accidents. But of all groups of patients, those with injuries sustained in fights and assaults had the highest percentage of positive readings, more than half.

Recently, a team from Johns Hopkins School of Public Health documented, for the first time, a link between drinking and drowning, disclosing that 47 percent of the drowning victims in one U.S. metropolitan area had positive blood alcohol tests. Mrs. Susan P. Baker, assistant professor of forensic pathology, and Park E. Dietz, doctoral student, told the American Public Health Association that twenty-one of forty-five adult drowning victims in Baltimore from 1968 to 1972 had positive blood alcohol concentrations, and seventeen were significantly intoxicated. Eleven of the intoxicated victims had been swimming, four fell from boats, two drowned in bathtubs, three stepped into deep water and one fell from a pier in a shipyard where he worked. Noting that previous studies had merely implied the connection between drinking and drowning, Dr. Dietz said, "In response to the need for public awareness, swimming and boating courses should emphasize the increased hazard of aquatic sports for people who have been drinking."

The automobile, as noted earlier, can play a key role in shortening our lifespans, particularly when the driver or the pedestrian has been drinking. It's not a new problem, either, as this 1904 editorial from the *Quarterly Journal of Inebriety* proves:

> We have received a communication containing a history of 25 fatal accidents occurring to automobile wagons. Fifteen persons occupying these wagons were killed outright, five more died two days later. A careful inquiry showed that in 19 of these accidents the driver had used spirits within an hour or more of the disaster. The other six drivers were all moderate drinkers, but it was not ascertained whether they had used spirits preceding the accidents.

That year, 375 more persons were to die in auto accidents, but it is not known how many had been using liquor.

The horseless carriage was a "new-fangled contraption" in those days, but today it's a way of life, a necessity. It is more powerful and faster. Couple those qualities with alcohol, even a small amount, and driving becomes a problem. Increase the amount of liquor and you increase your chances of causing an accident. Recent United States and Australian studies of some one thousand drivers killed in accidents have shown that at least 44 percent were drunk when the crashes occurred, with blood alcohol concentrations of .10 percent or higher.

Whether or not lowering the drinking age, as has been legislated in a number of states, will continue to boost the fatalities among young people who drink and drive cannot be answered at this time. Reports from several states indicate that many more teenagers are now involved in fatal and nonfatal automobile accidents than were before the legal age for drinking was lowered to eighteen. Some public safety officials believe, however, that the novelty of teenage drinking will eventually wear off, and that as teenagers become more used to drinking, much of the irresponsible drinking that leads to accidents will disappear. Officials are also counting on young people taking the time to learn as much as they can about alcohol and its effects—even though they may not yet be of legal drinking age—so that they won't become a statistic on a chart at the local police station some day.

Since it's obvious that murder is a means of shortening our normal lifespans, it is vital to note that most of the statistics show that alcohol is a factor in half the homicides committed in the United States. And the figure doesn't only apply to the last few years, a turbulent, violent time of increased street murder and assassination. A study done in Philadelphia in the late nineteen forties and early fifties found that liquor played a part in some 70 percent of 356 murders done by stabbing, kicking and beating, and in half of more than 200 murders committed with firearms and by other means.

However, no one can say for certain that these people who committed murder would not have done so if they had not been under the influence of liquor. Murder is committed for a variety of reasons—poverty, mental illness, anger and brain defects, to name but a few—and to say that alcohol causes a person to kill is putting it rather simply. "No drug, narcotic or alcoholic beverage presently known will, by itself, lead to violence," said the National Commission on Causes and Prevention of Violence in 1969. The commission added that these substances can, through abuse and misuse, facilitate behavior that may end in violence to people or property.

The relationship between alcohol and death, the NIAAA report points out, can be direct, as in an overdose of liquor. In 1970, 134 of 300 poison deaths investigated by the North Carolina Medical Examiner were directly caused by alcohol, prompting Dr. Abdullah Fatteh, professor of pathology at East Carolina University Medical School, to say: "Many people are not aware that alcohol in excess is poisonous and can kill." Or, the relationship can be indirect, as in the accidents we have been discussing, where the alcohol has produced a physical or mental state that puts the drinkers more at risk.

But, the government report adds:

It should be noted that even when an association is found between a particular pattern of drinking and mortality, it does not necessarily follow that the drinking caused death. The association may be due to some other factors which are common to both drinking and the deaths. From the point of view of public policy, the important issue is: Would the excess mortality disappear if the alcohol were removed from the situation? With the partial exception of the drunken-driving cases, much of the data on excess mortality is based on samples in which an elevated mortality is to be expected even in the absence of drinking.

In other words, determining the exact extent to which alcohol is truly and directly responsible for death is as difficult as determining how much it directly affects the body's various organs and causes disease. Data from insurance companies and a number of general population surveys suggest, however, that heavy and problem drinkers seem to live shorter lives, and that moderate drinkers live the longest. For some reason, abstainers—just as they may be struck by more heart attacks—seem to have a shorter life expectancy than moderate drinkers, though better than heavy drinkers.

Six

The Hangover

—◆◆◆—

LINDA: Alcohol, yuk! Getting drunk must be the worst feeling. No, I guess it isn't really, but it's pretty bad. I first got drunk the summer after sixth grade. My boyfriend and I used to go to dances, he'd get a half gallon of wine and we'd finish it in five minutes. My legs never held me up. I'd end up on the floor very confused with everything. It'd all be whirling around. I got tired of that. Maybe I don't need it anymore.

BOB: My first real experience drinking was in a cemetery. My friend ripped off a bottle of rum, a quart, from a kid and hid it under a pile of leaves near a tree. Both of us were pretty nervous about getting caught by some cop or being seen by people passing the cemetery because it was about 9:30 in the morning. We tried to empty out the bottle pretty fast, and after about a half hour the bottle was down a ways. When I got up I was staggering, but my friend was a little bit better. We walked for about an hour, and my balance got worse, and I started to get sick. On the way, I puked on the street. I got home and puked some more, maybe for two hours. Luckily my parents weren't home. My head buzzed until the next day. I learned that hard stuff and me didn't mix, so I decided to go with beer next time. A month later, I had eight beers and I smoked six bowls of pot. I wasn't staggering but when I got home I had the munchies. I ate a pile of food, and an hour later I was in the same condition as when I drank that rum. I was puking my brains out. Since then, no more for me. I smoke pot about once a week now. That way I get the euphoria but without getting sick. Drinking is okay, I suppose, as long as you don't get sick or become a down-and-outer.

———◆◆◆———

Many who have gotten sick after drinking too much probably have taken a solemn oath that they'd never do it again. It's a promise that most of them did not keep, if only because when unpleasantness and pain go away we tend to forget all the misery. And so we start out again as though nothing happened. But that, as they say, is human nature, and about all we can do in the case of drinking is try to avoid circumstances in which alcohol is the sole reason for getting together. If you do want to drink, then do it the right way.

One of the most celebrated effects of drinking the wrong way is the so-called hangover, and everyone should know about it even if they've never experienced it.

In the last chapter, we talked about some of the long-term results that come from drinking too much. The hangover is a short-term result, and usually comes on "the morning after the night before." If you haven't experienced its miseries—pounding headache, nausea and extreme fatigue—maybe you've been aware that some member of your family hasn't felt all that great the morning after a party.

Medicine doesn't really acknowledge that the hangover exists. You can't find it in a standard medical dictionary and few doctors will treat it, mostly because they don't know how. The majority of physicians, many of whom have been there themselves, simply laugh at the word, medicate little and moralize a lot. The hangover is a bit like the song some years ago about the little man who wasn't there—when he wasn't there again today, you'd wish he'd go far, far away.

Everyone has a favorite cure for the hangover, and there are as many as for hiccups. Most of them are concoctions that may have worked once for someone, but without any scientific or any other reason. Among the more ridiculous "cures" you'll hear and read about regularly are: yogurt mixed with strawberry jam, raw egg with hot pepper and steak sauce, warm milk with butter and yeast, raw oysters and horseradish, champagne and saltines. There's also no evidence that vitamins or drugs will do any good. One of the most widely-touted remedies is "the hair of the dog that bit you"—in other words, a morning-after drink of the same kind of liquor consumed the night before.

Some things can, however, be done to treat the variety of symptoms typical of morning-after, and there is no magic about them.

One authority who has taken a close look at the chemistry and physiology of the hangover is Dr. Donald J. Dalessio, head of the division of neurology at Scripps Clinic and Research Foundation in La Jolla, California.

First, Dr. Dalessio advised in an article in 1970 in *Medical Opinion and Review*, the headache should be attacked. Since it is related to overdilation of the blood vessels (alcohol dilates the vessels, particularly those in the head), one should attempt to constrict them. Medications that contain ergotamine are very helpful. (Ergot, derived from fungus, is used in prescription drugs.) Caffeine also constricts the blood vessels, and some pharmaceutical houses have put up remedies containing both caffeine and ergotamine. If nausea is a problem, Dr. Dalessio reported, these medications must be taken in the form of a rectal suppository.

Since alcohol also causes an increase in urine flow, the heavy drinker is dehydrated. Replacement of water alone will not help, since a water-loaded stomach may increase nausea and vomiting. A far more acceptable solution, according to the doctor, is salty broth. Upon arising with a hangover, several cups of well-salted broth may be taken and repeated several hours later if necessary. When the salt and water are replaced, nausea will decrease and the negative water balance straightened out. There is also some evidence that low blood sugar may be an important contributing factor, and broth provides a ready source of calories and is rapidly taken into the bloodstream. Orange juice is also a good source of water, minerals and calories, but should not be drunk if nausea is present since the citric acid may add fuel to that particular fire.

Ethyl alcohol is ordinarily metabolized in the body at a constant rate, but it is possible to modify this rate by eating certain foods, especially those containing the common sugar, fructose. So, by adding foods that contain fructose into the diet when drinking is contemplated, the alcohol may be burned off considerably faster.

Honey, says Dr. Dalessio, may be added to several different canapés. A slice of toast, well spread with honey, taken before bed after an evening of heavy drinking, is a simple and effective remedy. Vegetable juices ingested during the hangover hours are helpful in hastening the metabolism of whatever alcohol remains to be metabolized. "The standard morning-after cocktail of tomato juice and various added spices may be more sound than previously suspected by some observers," the doctor adds.

Position may also play a role in hangover headache, says the doctor. "The slack and dilated vessels that produce the headache may be considerably constricted by arising, even though one's senses suggest that one remain in bed." Ice applied to the head is a satisfactory way of constricting the vessels.

Regarding the "hair of the dog," Dr. Dalessio warns that taking a morning-after drink is a very dangerous practice. "The repeated ingestion of alcohol on first arising," he says, "may represent a prelude to the more serious problem of alcoholism, a complex socio-economic and psychiatric dilemma that continues to frustrate our society."

Insofar as its effectiveness is concerned, though many drinkers swear by "hair of the dog," there doesn't seem to be much scientific proof that it is a curative. One 1974 study involving two subjects, however, did demonstrate that morning drinking helped relieve suffering. "Barroom mythology has asserted that a hefty nip in the morning after alcoholic overindulgence can give a measure of relief," Dr. James B. Hoon of the Sheboygan Clinic in Wisconsin reported in the *Journal of the American Medical Association*. "Opportunity to test this hypothesis arose while I was doing gastrocamera testing of drugs. One of my experimental subjects, age twenty-two years, had made the observation that if his stomach 'looks like my eyeballs you're really going to see something this morning.' " The young man had consumed a good deal of alcohol the night before and had a hangover on the morning of the study. Photos with the gastrocamera taken of the inside of his stomach showed much turmoil and acid secretion. The subject was then given one-and-a-half ounces of 90-proof gin, and more pictures were taken. This time they showed a definitely calmer stomach.

Dr. Hoon got a similar result with another patient, a twenty-five-year-old man who had attended his brother's wedding reception the previous night. "I do not advocate morning drinking," Dr. Hoon concluded. "I merely point out that in the two subjects presented, it worked to relieve suffering and I have some gastrocamera evidence of this point."

In the last analysis, the best remedy is to avoid the hangover in the first place. The way to do that is to sip slowly in relaxing circumstances, with food in the stomach. And, of course, avoid getting drunk.

Seven

Treatment

❖❖❖

SARAH: You can't say I really drink. But when I do once in
a while I drink for the challenge. I want to know how I
feel when I'm drunk. The challenge of smoking is gone,
and that was a bad experience. So maybe you can write in
your book that it's a challenge, an experience. Life is made
up of finding out.

❖❖❖

In 1974, The Joint Committee on Health Problems in
Education of the National Education Association and
the American Medical Association adopted the following
resolution on alcohol and health:

Whereas,   A major problem in the U.S.A. is the
           abuse of alcohol, and
Whereas,   Accidents, many disease processes, and
           other psychological and physiological
           complications result from the injudicious
           use of alcohol, and
Whereas,   Some educators and physicians are un-
           aware of or unaccepting of these facts,
           and
Whereas,   Many medical colleges offer inadequate
           instruction concerning the problems asso-
           ciated with the use of alcohol, and
Whereas,   Teacher education seldom includes an un-
           derstanding either of appropriate uses of
           alcohol or of problems related to the use
           of alcohol, therefore be it

Resolved,   That educators and physicians seek
              continuing education, including self-
              education, to increase their understand-
              ing of the use of alcohol; and be it further
Resolved,   That physicians and educators vigorously
              seek ways to communicate to the public,
              including the schools, pertinent informa-
              tion about the use and abuse of alcohol;
              and be it further
Resolved,   That both professions seek ways of help-
              ing communities face the fact that the
              abuse of alcohol cannot be solved in a
              punitive manner, but requires dissemina-
              tion of correct information and a realistic
              and sympathetic attitude toward the total
              problem.

The last resolve, that alcohol abuse cannot be solved in a punitive manner, points up an enlightened attitude that has emerged only in recent years. Alcoholics are not sinful people but sick people whose sickness might force them to act immorally. If they are guilty of any willful wrongdoing, it is generally only that they may refuse to seek help. And they may have no control over that either, just as they have no control over their drinking.

Like mental illness or physical disease, alcoholism is not a state that one can bring on deliberately, nor does it usually explode all of a sudden in a nonalcoholic individual after several drinks at a wild party. Alcoholism is more complicated than that, as we have seen; the sufferer only loses control of himself or herself after several years of problem drinking.

Though some myths, misconceptions and hypocritical moralizing still surface from time to time, and though medical and mental health professionals sometimes ignore the problem either out of ignorance, disinterest or lack of funds for treatment programs, an increasing number of states are passing laws removing public drunkenness and alcoholism from the list of criminal offenses. No longer are the intoxicated punished by locking them in a "drunk-ard's cloak," a tub with holes for the arms to pass through, as was done in the seventeenth century. And one would like to believe, at least, that in many parts of the country the local jail is not as it was described in the textbook for a college course in criminology back in the fifties:

> The jail today still serves the same functions as it did in Colonial times. It is still a place of detention for those awaiting trial, its original function; a prison for the incarceration of misdemeanants and petty offenders, and a "parking place" for vagrants. Besides, most jails house those who are suffering from chronic alcoholism or from the effects of narcotics, prostitutes, and panderers, shiftless derelicts, material witnesses and others of heterogeneous nature. The promiscuity and the utter lack of segregation of the contemporary jail are two of its worst features. Especially serious, too, is the intermingling of first offenders, in most cases boys and young men, with older and more degraded types of depraved persons and adepts in petty crime and debauchery.

Chief Judge Elijah Adlow of the Boston Municipal Court put it aptly at a hearing held by a special commission on mental health in 1965. "In my opinion," the outspoken judge said, "the time has come for the legislature to brand alcoholism as a disease and to provide for it as such. Legislation must be passed requiring the compulsory commitment of all alcoholics who have been arrested more than four times in the previous twelve months. The commitment should not be to the local jail or house of correction but to the Bridgewater State Farm which should operate under the joint supervision of the Department of Mental Diseases and the Department of Correction. The term of commitment should be six months, with the right of earlier release in the discretion of the doctors. The inmates should be patients, not prisoners. Half the resistance to whatever treatment that is provided now comes from parents and friends who dread the criminal label. These men are not criminals and should not be treated as such. Let's end the absurd situation in which judges are prescribing cures for a disease."

There is little doubt that the atmosphere of moral disapproval that has hung about alcoholism, and the imprisoning of alcoholics as perverts or criminals, has done much to obscure the nature of the problem. "No other national

91

health problem has been so seriously neglected as alcoholism," HEW Secretary John Gardner said some years ago. "Many doctors decline to accept alcoholics as patients. Most hospitals refuse to admit alcoholics. Available methods of treatment have not been widely applied. Research on alcoholism and excessive drinking has received virtually no significant support."

That situation seems to have changed somewhat for the better, according to Caspar W. Weinberger, HEW Secretary in 1974:

> There was a time not many years ago when alcohol abuse and alcoholism were not considered important problems. As a nation, we turned our backs on what we now recognize as a serious problem. Both as a government official and as a citizen, I am pleased to say that Americans are no longer ignoring the unfortunate consequences that result from the misuse of alcohol.

In 1968, in a sharply divided decision, the United States Supreme Court refused to extend the Eighth Amendment's ban against "cruel and unusual" punishment to those who get drunk in public. This meant, put another way, that chronic alcoholics might be jailed without violating their constitutional rights and that chronic alcoholism is not a defense against public drunkenness. "We are unable to conclude," Justice Thurgood Marshall said in delivering the 5–4 opinion,

> on the state of this record or on the current state of medical knowledge, that chronic alcoholics in general ... suffer from such an irresistible compulsion to get drunk in public that they are utterly unable to control their performance of either or both of these acts and thus cannot be deterred at all from public intoxication. It is simply not yet the time to write into the Constitution formulas cast in terms whose meaning, let alone relevance, are not yet clear to doctors or to lawyers.

Fears were expressed in the prevailing opinion that applying the unusual punishment bar to drunkenness might undermine the ancient principles of common law that hold an individual responsible for a criminal act. Also, the judge warned, the law might conceivably be stretched further to defend those who commit, say, murder while drunk. The dissenting opinion was written by Justice Abe Fortas, who pointed out that alcoholism is a disease that takes away the will to remain sober. Punishing the alcoholic for being drunk in public, he added, is punishing that person for something he or she cannot help or change. The decision did not prevent states from setting up laws making alcoholism a defense against drunkenness and, in effect, allowing it to be considered a medical problem. In Massachusetts, which no longer regards drunkenness as a crime, Elliot L. Richardson, then state attorney general, said the Supreme Court decision meant simply that the high court was not prepared to tell all the states that alcoholism was not a crime. The individual states, he said, were free to pursue a more humane approach.

Alcoholism can be treated, and problem drinking can be avoided. But since the disease has so many faces, not all the methods of treatment work with every patient. Treatment has to be tailored to each alcoholic according to his or her needs and also to what is available in a community. Often, as in treating mental illness, a combination of several forms of therapy is most helpful. Some, we shall see a bit later, even mirror therapies used to treat the mentally ill, such as group and aversion therapy. Drugs may be used, but it must be stressed that none can actually cure alcoholism; when they are stopped, the problem remains—though there is some difference of opinion over whether a recovered alcoholic can return to safe drinking at a later date.

Everyone probably knows someone with a problem involving liquor. It could be a close friend, parents, a neighbor, or even oneself. Sometimes, the people who do have a problem don't do anything about it. It may be because they are unaware that something can be done about it, or where it can be done. Fear or embarrassment may keep some people from seeking help. Sometimes, relatives try to protect a family member by avoiding the issue, an understandable approach but one that might mean killing an alcoholic with kindness since the disease is fatal if left to heal itself. Or, it may simply be that people don't think

93

about alcoholism as a problem; they might feel that all those times they've been bombed didn't have to happen because they can stop any time they want.

Maybe some people can stop at will, but chances are if they get drunk a lot, if they can't have fun without it, or they do it when they're on a down, it won't be that easy. What's even sadder is that a lot of the people who see other people in trouble with liquor aren't going to do much to help because they still don't understand that people with a drinking problem are not sinful people. Maybe you've felt that way yourself about problem drinkers. Sometimes, we do have a tendency to think that sick people—particularly mentally ill individuals or addicts of all kinds—are beneath us, and we get angry at them because they are that way.

Both professionals and laypersons, the NIAAA report tells us, see the alcoholic as a person who "chooses" to drink and therefore becomes trapped in alcoholism. Since alcoholics get themselves into the mess they're in, according to this argument, it is their responsibility to get out of it by "lifting themselves out by their bootstraps." Thus, nothing can be done to treat them unless they take the first step themselves.

"It is paradoxical, yet understandable," says the government report, "that the alcoholic person is thought to act with intent and choice, when in fact the essential characteristic of his illness is that he is disabled from directing his actions, especially where alcohol is concerned. It is notable that successful alcoholism programs are those that have an aggressive outreach. Alcoholic persons do respond to treatment alternatives when they are offered."

Twenty-five or thirty years ago, there were few facilities for the treatment of alcoholics. Connecticut, in 1943, became the first state to provide medical care for them. Today, throughout the nation, there are many programs, facilities and agencies to help the person with a drinking problem. These include alcoholism information and referral centers, general and mental hospitals, alcoholism rehabilitation hospitals, detoxification programs, tuberculosis hospitals, veterans' hospitals, halfway houses, vocational rehabilitation clinics, alcoholism outpatient clinics, private physicians, skid row agencies, community human service agencies, business and industrial rehabilitation programs, the police-court system, Alcoholics Anonymous, Al-Anon and Al-Ateen.

In dealing with the ability to treat alcoholism, the American Medical Association points out that because the illness is a chronic one—that is, one of long duration—with a tendency toward relapse, the aim of treatment should be one of control rather than cure. "Abstinence is sought as a prime objective," the AMA advises,

> but additional considerations, such as improved social or occupational adjustments, may be far better guides in evaluating the success or failure of a treatment effort. Temporary relapse with return to drinking, then, should not be equated with failure, any more than should the diabetic's occasional discontinuation of his diet or his insulin. The goal of every program should be to help the alcohol-dependent patient learn to deal effectively with his life problems without using the drug and to adapt to his environment in a reasonably mature manner. At the same time, the effort should be to prevent or correct the complications of his illness. Treatment centers which have utilized this approach have achieved quite remarkable success in the management of many alcoholic patients. There seems to be no good reason why these results cannot be duplicated by others, including individual physicians.

While total and permanent abstinence is the goal of most programs, this end can be very difficult to achieve for the alcoholic whose "thirst" for liquor is as unbearable as that of the junkie for heroin. Some specialists maintain that only about 20 percent of all treated patients are able to remain abstinent for more than three to five years. Some place the figure higher. At the recent North American Congress on Alcohol and Drug Problems, it was reported that therapy is still helpful even though it does not lead to abstinence. One group from the Hazledon Foundation in Minnesota found that the lives of former patients improved, even though they still drink.

Keeping all of this in mind—along with the fact that alcoholism is a complex disorder that has been characterized as "one part physical, one part psychological, one part sociological and one part alcohol"—let's examine some of the methods of treating it—excluding treatment of such specific alcohol-related ailments as cirrhosis, fatty liver and pancreatitis.

Treatment of the alcoholic may be handled by medical and nonmedical specialists. Contrary to the popular view, it is not only psychiatrists and psychologists who try to help the problem drinker. Thus, the kind of treatment often reflects the therapist's view of what causes alcoholism. A psychiatrist, for instance, might feel that alcoholism is surely a symptom of some emotional problem and tries to treat that. The person who believes that there is a physical cause of alcoholism, that the craving arises from some physical defect, will treat the patient accordingly. In either case, however, there is a danger of too much emphasis on one cause, which can lead to neglect of others that may play a part in the case. The alcoholic isn't helped as he or she should be, and those concerned over the drinker's welfare are frustrated and disappointed.

Psychotherapy on an individual basis or in groups is often employed in a treatment program. Individual therapy (one psychiatrist, one patient) can be costly and is not for all alcoholics. However, one form of individual therapy that may be useful is called supportive. The therapist uses reassurance, advice, persuasion, suggestion and inspiration to strengthen the patient. Such an approach does not probe too deeply into the root of the problem as does the more aggressive psychoanalysis which helps a patient bare his or her soul and then, hopefully, go on to restructure thinking and behavior.

Group therapy, which has proven to be quite effective and is at the core of many treatment programs, enables the patient to identify with others who have similar problems. By meeting regularly in groups, the alcoholic begins to understand himself or herself better, and also learns how to cope without alcohol. There are many ways of handling groups. Some combine both individual and group therapy, some allow the patient to drink if it is desired, with the hope that group persuasion will eventually make the alcoholic choose not to. Some are interested in why the patient drinks, others are not. But whatever the psychotherapy, the primary goal is usually to help the drinker change a drinking pattern and handle problems without the irresponsible use of liquor. Once the alcoholic acknowledges that he or she needs help, emphasis is placed on how drinking can be halted. Later, there may be efforts to get at the underlying reasons behind the drinking. It is not an easy road, particularly for the skid-row alcoholic who lacks the support of family, job and community ties that are so important on the way to recovery. The total abstinence from liquor which is included in most programs is, as we have said, most difficult, and the craving can be overpowering. Most clinicians feel that once an alcoholic gives up liquor, he or she can never return to using it in a moderate way. Not everyone agrees with that assessment, however. Some years ago, a group from the University of Cincinnati College of Medicine and the Alcoholism Clinic of the Cincinnati Health Department reported that some alcoholics apparently do manage to return to normal drinking. Of thirty-two ex-alcoholics studied at least a year after clinic treatment, eleven were totally abstinent, ten were compulsive drinkers and eleven were classified as "normal" drinkers. The researchers suggested that some persons may be alcoholic for reasons that can be changed with treatment. They also pointed out that abstinence in itself does not necessarily mean overall improvement in a patient because neuroses or other problems may remain even though the person has quit drinking.

Cure rates, of course, depend on many factors; these include the kind of treatment, motivation and intelligence of the patient. More often, specialists will measure a "cure" in terms of rehabilitation—in other words, the treatment is successful when the patient maintains or reestablishes a good family life and working habits, and is able to control drinking most of the time. Psychotic alcoholics, those with severe mental illness, are obviously not rehabilitated as readily as the average alcoholic since they cannot cooperate easily. It's been estimated that a successful outcome may be expected in those who are amenable to treatment and who have all other factors in their favor, in about 60 to 80 percent of cases. It is doubtful, though, whether any particular figure means much in itself. What is important is that the programs can and do work, depending on the determination of the patient to get well and the competence of the therapist.

"The lesson for the rehabilitation people is clear," Dr. Morris Chafetz told the Twenty-first National Institute on Crime and Delinquency in Boston in 1974. "If you treat an individual as he is, he will stay as he is. But if you treat him as what he can be and ought to be, he will become somebody with a set of values around which to build his life and protect his future."

Some physicians use a technique called aversion or behavior therapy to treat alcoholics. It is based on the classic experiments of Ivan Pavlov (1849–1936), a Russian scientist noted for his work in the field of conditioned reflexes. Pavlov offered food to dogs while he rang a bell at the same time. The dogs, whose mouths naturally watered every time the food was brought out, eventually also salivated when the bell was rung without food. The bell was the conditioned stimulus, the salivation the conditioned response. Behavior therapy treats human beings somewhat like animals in the sense that they can be trained or taught to rid themselves of undesirable behavior, such as heavy drinking. The bad habits are merely something that the patient has learned somehow. Aversion therapists might give an alcoholic a powerful nausea-producing drug like emetine, and then a shot of liquor. The alcoholic vomits, and after this combination is administered a few more times, associates the nausea, an unpleasant experience, with the liquor. The patient develops a conditioned reflex of disgust for even the sight of liquor. Sometimes, a jolt of electricity with a drink of liquor. There is considerable disagreement over whether such treatment provides any long-lasting cure; also, because there is danger of serious physical reaction, the treatment must be carefully supervised by medical specialists. Many patients also drop out of this type of treatment because it is quite unpleasant.

Some interesting work with alcoholics and conditioned response was reported in the British quarterly *Behavior Therapy* a few years ago, by Dr. Halmuth A. Schaefer, a professor of clinical psychiatry at Loma Linda University School of Medicine in California. Dr. Schaefer and his associates at that time had successfully treated close to a thousand alcoholics at Patton State Hospital. The group found, contrary to what many clinicians and others believe, that alcoholism is primarily a psychological illness, although it may have physiological results. The researchers also did not believe that alcoholics are weak willed with no power to stop drinking once they have started.

Dr. Schaefer and his team investigated the ordinary situations that apparently triggered the binge drinking of their alcoholic patients. They concluded that drink for these individuals was a conditioned response to anxiety. The alcoholic had learned, the team reasoned, that in times of stress, liquor is a quick relaxer and will relieve anxiety. (Recall, on the other hand, Dr. Mendelson's work in which it was found that alcoholics become depressed rather than less anxious with drink.) Thus, the alcoholic can be "cured" by learning a different but just as effective behavior in the same situation. Stress also may explain why so many alcoholics relapse after leaving the peace and quiet of an institution.

"We tried many forms of stress—insults, confrontation by video tape (letting the alcoholic see himself or herself at their worst on TV film), deliberate embarrassment, giving the alcoholic tasks he could not complete—and we found that, sure enough, under such conditions, he would have only one response, to reach for a glass," said Dr. Schaefer. "Our control subjects, who were 'social' drinkers, would respond in other ways. They'd get angry, eat too much, punch something, do physical exercise, but they didn't start drinking. The only reasonable assumption I can make is that the alcoholic learned this response before."

Genetic and physiologic factors may also be involved, the Loma Linda psychologist conceded, but they seem to be far less important than the effect of an immediate reward. "The alcoholic has learned that when he feels bad and takes a drink, he forgets that he feels bad. The hangovers, the sickness, the loss of job and family—they come much later on and are not part of taking the drink," he reported.

Treatment developed through this research first teaches the alcoholic why he or she drinks to excess. Each patient has a unique reason. "By talking to him and his relatives and by psychological tests, we get a list of the things that stress him. We recreate the occasions when he started to drink in the past, and a simple pattern emerges." After learning this disturbing lesson, the patient also learns, in a series of structured three-hour sessions lasting a month, other more reasonable behavior for situations which previously set off the drinking bouts.

The patient is given the choice of being an abstainer or a social drinker, one who can sip a drink or idle with a glass while sitting and chatting. If the patient joins Alcoholics Anonymous or faithfully belongs to a religious group which will support abstention, this goal can be successful. If abstention has previously failed, however, and is likely to fail again because the patient's social and work environment evidently provides too much counter-pressure, the patient is instead taught a whole new behavior pattern. This might be how to be a fastidious gourmet instead of a gulper of liquor. With that aim, the investigators set up an appropriate research setting—one that is especially familiar to alcoholics. A cocktail lounge was recreated in Patton State Hospital for these lessons, dimly lit, with mirrored bar, sentimental jukebox music, liquor provided by the Alcoholic Beverage Control Board from confiscated goods, and even the stale, rancid smells common to such places were simulated.

"It's quite necessary," Dr. Schaefer explained, "because we want to extinguish the alcoholic behavior under the same conditions in which it occurs. Otherwise what happens outside would be different, and the patient would relapse when he got out of the hospital."

In the course of treatment, the psychologists used videotapes of their patients and of control groups, but in very mild scenes; they show the alcoholics what they would not otherwise have believed—how their behavior differs from social drinking. For instance, they prefer straight to mixed drinks, finish the drinks faster, in huge swallows, although pausing longer between such swallows than the social drinker does between sips; and they continue drinking well beyond the stage at which the social drinker would have stopped.

Finally, the volunteer patient, deterred by painful but harmless electric shock to the fingers when too many drinks are consumed quickly, learns to copy the social drinker's behavior pattern. Weak, mixed drinks are taken and the technique of sipping is acquired. Most important, the alcoholic learns several socially acceptable ways of refusing more.

Filming of alcoholics and then showing them the pictures, as was done in Dr. Schaefer's work, was reported also a few years earlier by a psychiatrist from Jefferson Medical College of Philadelphia at a meeting of the American Medical Association. Dr. Alfonso Paredes took movies of alcoholics while they were intoxicated, then screened them for their benefit when they sobered up. Some of the patients were so shaken by the experience that they stopped drinking. "For the first time," Dr. Paredes said, "the alcoholic, the most important person, sees himself as others have been seeing him for years." Dr. Schaefer has pointed out that using such a self-confrontation technique could provide too much stress and be harmful. He cautioned that video playback alone, without any other therapy, should not be used with alcoholics since it could induce rather than suppress renewed drinking.

Dr. John A. Renner, director of the Alcohol Clinic at Massachusetts General Hospital, has said that for some patients the film experience is clearly very useful. "But most people just wouldn't come back," he observed recently in the *MGH News*. "It was probably too confronting, too quickly. Most people, because of what they are like when drunk, blot out how they behaved and have all sorts of fantasies about how they acted, but these have little basis for reality."

Among the more successful treatment programs is that at the Johnson Institute in Minneapolis. It has worked, according to its founder, Vernon E. Johnson, for seven out of ten who have been exposed to it. Basically, the therapy is designed to bring the patient back to reality. Each alcoholic who comes into the program undergoes about four weeks of intensive care in a hospital for his or her acute symptoms, then up to two years of aftercare as an outpatient. Annual studies at St. Mary's Hospital in Minnesota, one of the backup institutions used by the institute, indicate that some 52 percent of patients never drink again after completing the program. The other 48 percent, according to Johnson, relapse and experiment with liquor. But about half of these dropouts return and complete the outpatient program successfully and, according to Johnson, remain abstinent.

The first goal of the inpatient treatment is to get the alcoholic physically freed of chemicals. Then, through weeks of intensive therapy, the individual gains an understanding of his destructive behavior and defense system patterns which keep him locked into the vicious cycle. The alcoholic must learn, possibly for the first time, how to feel good about himself. For many, the treatment is the beginning of the question, "Who am I?" During the outpatient portion, one-to-one counseling, group therapy and Alcoholics Anonymous complement each other, and together they help the individual to achieve a contented sobriety.

Pharm House, sponsored by the Johnson Institute, helps young people deal with alcohol and drug dependency and put their lives back together. There is a crisis center and a treatment center. The crisis center offers outpatient groups, family groups, crisis intervention, information sessions and a speakers bureau. Analysis and identification of drugs are offered to help users avoid poisoning and overdosing. The treatment center offers a long-term program, about six months, and is said to be unusually effective for young chemical dependents.

Pharm House has chosen the following inspirational lines by the ancient Chinese philosopher Lao Tzu to draw attention to its approach:

There is no need
To run outside
For better seeing
Nor to peer
From a window
Rather abide
At the center
Of your being
For the more
You leave it
The less you learn
Search your heart
And see
If he is wise
Who takes each turn
The way to go
Is to be.

A key element in the treatment of alcoholics is awareness by employers of the scope of the problem. Realizing that alcoholic male workers are responsible for the loss of at least nine billion dollars ($9 billion) a year in goods and services, hundreds of firms and federal agencies such as the U. S. Postal Service are cooperating in their treatment; they're also trying to help detect the problem in its early stages. One estimate cited in the NIAAA report indicates that at least 2.6 million people work in organizations that offer some degree of formal help for problem drinkers and other employees whose work performance is below average. Labor unions are also often involved in these programs, and coverage for the costs of treatment is included in a growing number of company medical insurance policies. According to a recent report by the Health Insurance Institute, a survey of seventeen major insurance companies writing group disability income insurance in the United States found that all of them will cover loss of income resulting from alcoholism. Until recently, insurance benefits for disability were not paid for loss of time due to alcoholism. The more recent acceptance of alcoholism as an illness has brought about the change in the insurance companies' attitudes.

There is, however, usually the proviso that the alcoholic's condition should be medically recognized, and the alcoholic must be placed under medical supervision. The insurance policies state that disability benefits will not begin until the alcoholic has agreed to undergo treatment to overcome the drinking problem. Once the benefits begin, they continue only as long as the alcoholic continues treatment and rehabilitation. Should treatment be discontinued, benefits stop. "Since 60% to 80% of employed alcoholics have been shown to respond favorably to treatment," says J. F. Follmann, Jr., consultant to the NIAAA, "the approach taken by insurance companies benefits the employer, fellow employees and certainly the individual and his family." (The 80 percent success rate claimed for industry compares favorably with the results of general treatment of most psychiatric illness.)

One example of how industry participates in a treatment program may be found in New Hampshire, which has one of the highest per capita consumption rates of alcohol in the nation. Although actual statistics are difficult to come by, a rough estimate is that about five percent of the population—one person in twenty—is alcoholic. Within the primary service area covered by the alcohol treatment program of the Dartmouth-Hitchcock Mental Health Center, a division of Mary Hitchcock Memorial Hospital, it is estimated that there are approximately three thousand alcoholics. Loss to industry due to alcoholism, therefore, is high in the area. There are, according to the center, well over one thousand employed alcoholics in its service area; they cost their employers over $1.5 million a year as a result of absenteeism, sick leave, wasted time and material and accidents.

In response to this problem, the alcohol treatment program recently surveyed some twenty-one industries to assess both management's and personnel's understanding of the alcohol problem. The alcohol team has been working with two area industrial groups to develop effective educational and treatment programs for industry. Furthermore, the team is already making their resources available to other community organizations.

The program is staffed by an interdisciplinary team of psychiatrists, social workers, psychologists, a vocational counselor, an activities therapist, an alcoholism counselor and public health nurses. They are available for consultation and collaboration with the professional staff of the medical center as well as community physicians and community organizations. In addition, the team provides direct consultation to individuals and their families. The alcohol team is available directly on weekdays by telephone through the hospital in their offices at the mental health center. They also receive referrals from the mental health center's emergency walk-in service, the hospital emergency department, and from the various inpatient and outpatient services of the medical center. Members of the treatment team and other trained persons are available to talk with interested groups, large or small. They also provide a bibliography of available literature and recommend other sources of information about alcohol and alcohol-related problems.

"The real goal of the program," according to Dr. Robert Chapman, staff psychiatrist, "is to form effective ties with the medical community, business, industry, schools, social organizations and government in order to inform and educate the community about alcoholism and form a community-wide plan for the early recognition and effective treatment of those individuals who are affected physically, socially or emotionally by their continued use of alcohol."

Another approach is the joint venture among Middlesex County Hospital, Metropolitan State Hospital and the Walter E. Fernald State School, all in Massachusetts. It is a cooperative effort by county and state agencies, and private businesses have requested that they be included. The program works on two levels. A six-week seminar for supervisors points to alcoholism as an illness, not as a moral question, and offers ways for the supervisors to help alcoholic employees at the three hospitals. The employees with a drinking problem are offered counseling, with no mention of the problem entered in their personnel records. They are also urged to take advantage of established agencies and organizations designed to help alcoholics.

After completing their third seminar series, the program administrators felt they had some good results. There had been a drop in the number of industrial accidents, and employees' morale had improved because one employee did not have to make up for the work of another who had been drinking.

According to the NIAAA report, the U.S. Postal Service was the first federal government agency to start a formal program aimed at assisting the problem drinker to recover. The program was designed as a complete system; it dealt with the identification, treatment, education and follow-up of employees with a drinking problem. "Action" rather than clinically oriented, the program uses as its foundation the fulltime counseling services of recovered alcoholic persons. The system, according to the NIAAA, has effectively assisted three out of every four persons who participated, for a total of over three thousand, and is now being expanded to cover all installations in the postal service.

Considerable progress, according to the government report, has also been made in the development of programs for both military and civilian employees of the Department of Defense. The several branches of the military have developed policy statements and plans for dealing with problem drinking which are oriented toward help rather than punishment or dismissal. The army has instituted combined problem-drinking and drug-abuse programs at numerous installations in the United States and abroad, with emphasis on identifying those whose work has suffered, and providing on-base counseling. The navy has moved forward with two types of referral and treatment approaches. The first consists of regional rehabilitation centers to deal with problem drinkers who require a comprehensive treatment program. The second is made up of "dry docks" located on navy bases and designed for relatively brief treatment of identified problem drinkers. Both approaches include a strong emphasis on Alcoholics Anonymous as a major source of help and for follow-up maintenance.

Psychiatrists and others who deal with drinking problems have generally believed that if treatment is to succeed it must be voluntary. Industrial programs may be one example of how involuntary treatment can work. Says the MGH's Dr. Renner: "Once the large companies become aware of a drinking problem which is affecting the work capacity of an employee, they give him the choice of getting treatment or possibly losing his job. Most choose therapy."

Another involuntary treatment that can succeed is through a special program funded by the U. S. Department of Transportation to help persons convicted of drunken driving. The overwhelming majority of drunken drivers, many of them young people, are alcoholics. Known as the Alcoholism Safety Action Project (ASAP), the program has been tested in selected cities. By agreement with the courts in these cities, persons convicted of drunken driving did not receive the usual mandatory license suspension. Rather, they were given a choice: either enter treatment or have their licenses suspended. When the mandatory suspension was in effect, police were reluctant to arrest offenders and courts to convict them. Both knew that if the drivers lost their licenses, they might also lose their jobs, their homes and their families. As a result, the law's stiff penalty failed to deter the alcoholic who would return to the road again, even after several arrests. While the ASAP was in effect, yearly drunk-driving fatalities decreased 32 percent in the Boston area. In unaffected portions of Massachusetts, meanwhile, such deaths increased.

"The individuals who entered treatment under this program were coerced," Dr. Renner observes. "They came into therapy angry and hostile. They didn't want to be there, and they denied they had a problem." Yet, with many of these people, treatment succeeded.

A number of agencies are involved in treating alcoholics and caring for their families. Among the oldest are the Salvation Army, the Volunteers of America and many church-sponsored missions. The Woman's Christian Temperance Union, too, despite the jokes and jibes often aimed at it, and in spite of its hard-line approach, has helped in its own way. Though some of the programs offer chiefly spiritual assistance, a growing number use the services of psychiatrists and other medical specialists.

Probably the best known and most effective of the helping-hand agencies is Alcoholics Anonymous (AA), a fellowship of some seven hundred thousand alcoholics that began in 1935. Members help themselves and one another in a group therapy setting of comradeship and honesty.

They freely admit their drinking problems and describe their personal experiences, getting not lectures and speeches at their meetings but understanding, sympathy and encouragement. They believe that while alcoholism is not a happy state, it is not a disgrace. The only requirement for membership is a desire to quit drinking. There are no dues or fees, and AA is not allied with any religious denomination, political organization or institution. "Our primary purpose is to stay sober," says its introductory literature, "and help other alcoholics to achieve sobriety."

AA has chosen to identify alcoholism as an allergy resembling the situation of a diabetic with a craving for sugar. The organization, at the same time, agrees that any of the other theories about cause may be true in whole or in part. Contrary to what many people believe, AA members often do cooperate with therapists in other health professions since the AA program may not work completely for all alcoholics. "Our case histories," says AA, "prove that if a person definitely decides to give up drinking, and if he is not mentally impaired, no failure is possible, provided he honestly and energetically follows the program."

The so-called Twelve Steps of AA (which also have been translated to be used as a treatment for drug addicts) sum up what the organization believes to be the way to recovery. Based on experiences of members and not on the theories and book learning of physicians, sociologists or clergymen who have never known the anguish of a severe drinking problem, they are rules of conduct worth reading even by those who are not alcoholics or who do not know any:

1. We admitted we were powerless over alcohol, that our lives had become unmanageable.
2. Came to believe that a power greater than ourselves could restore us to sanity.
3. Made a decision to turn our will and our lives over to the care of God *as we understand Him*.
4. Made a searching and fearless moral inventory of ourselves.
5. Admitted to God, to ourselves, and to another human being the exact nature of our wrongs.
6. Were entirely ready to have God remove all these defects of character.
7. Humbly asked Him to remove our shortcomings.

8. Made a list of all persons we had harmed, and became willing to make amends to them all.

9. Made direct amends to such people wherever possible, except when to do so would injure them or others.

10. Continued to take personal inventory and when we were wrong promptly admitted it.

11. Sought through prayer and meditation to improve our conscious contact with God *as we understand Him* praying only for knowledge of His will for us and the power to carry that out.

12. Having had a spiritual experience as the result of these steps, we tried to carry this message to alcoholics, and to practice these principles in all our affairs.

The steps are not "musts" but suggestions to be tried. Members understand, too, that probably only a saint could practice all of them rigidly. "But years of experience have shown that we can take a few of them in a comparatively short time and thus start changing our unmanageable lives to lives of usefulness and happiness," the AA points out.

A key element in AA is the twenty-four-hour program, which is simply this:

We ask the Power that we recognize as being greater than ourselves (in most cases God as we understand God) in the morning to help us go through twenty-four hours without a drink. And at the end of the day, we thank that Power for helping us. The next day the same procedure is followed. It is repeated each succeeding day until we find that these 24-hour periods have grown to weeks and months, our thinking is clearer and we are better able to consider practicing more of the 12 steps in our daily lives. It might be difficult in your present state of mind to realize that your thinking has anything to do with your drinking. But we have found this to be so.

Many therapists see AA as a valuable adjunct to any treatment, but not as a substitute for all types of treatment.

With much of the attention focused on the country's millions of alcoholics, too often the 36 million people who are touched and even injured by the alcoholism of family members are neglected. To remedy that imbalance—and it is a serious matter because living with an alcoholic can be a most trying and painful experience—increasing efforts are being made to involve the family in the treatment process. One organization, Al-Anon, helps the wives and husbands of alcoholics, using techniques like that of AA. Al-Ateen helps the children of alcoholics understand their parents' problems, and Al-Atots aids the younger children of alcoholics. The purpose is to better the home environment, thereby improving the alcoholic's chances of recovery.

A program at Butler Hospital in Providence, Rhode Island, is an example of how an alcoholic and the alcoholic's spouse are both treated. Because spouses will often deny that alcoholism in their partner is an illness, mental or physical, those in charge of the project allow the couple to spend every day together in therapy to show what living with an alcoholic under treatment is like. "In effect, what we are doing is treating both the alcoholic and the person close to him," Dr. Thomas J. Paolini, director of the project, has said. "By watching how the hospital staff deals with the patient, the wife or husband will gain a better understanding of how to deal with the illness." The hospital staff also has the opportunity to talk to the spouse frequently, and may even find that some marital difficulty caused the drinking problem.

It has been demonstrated in several other programs as well that the wives and husbands of alcoholics may need group therapy themselves because of some neurosis brought on by their mate's problem. Teenagers also might get into difficulty—crime, running away from home, or into drugs—because their alcoholic parent or parents cannot guide them properly. Group sessions often help these teens to cope with their own problems as well as allow them to deal more adequately with their attitudes toward alcoholism and the alcoholic.

A number of drugs have been tried in the treatment of alcoholism. Already mentioned was medication that makes the alcoholic nauseous if liquor is drunk after it is taken. Tranquilizers are sometimes administered to relax the alcoholic and to quiet the tensions and anxieties that may have led to the drinking problem.

But for a great many patients, such measures provide only temporary relief. One widely used deterrent drug

(Antabuse) is an example. While the patient is on the drug, drinking alcohol in any form whatsoever—even in cough syrup or sauces—triggers pounding headache, violent nausea, vomiting and flushing. The manufacturer, Ayerst Laboratories, advertises in medical journals that Antabuse is "social security for the alcoholic who wants to stop drinking." Then it offers this sound piece of advice to the physician who reads the ad and is responsible for prescribing the drug:

> While he's on Antabuse, you can give the chronic alcoholic the support he needs to persist in the medical program. And, of course, you know the importance of reminding patients of the serious consequences of drinking while on Antabuse. Once sober, the alcoholic can participate in a total treatment program which makes use of various supportive resources in the community such as concerned organizations and the clergy. In the meantime, Antabuse can help the chronic alcoholic abstain from drinking.

Another drug currently being tried is lithium, an alkali metal that is used in such nonmedical endeavors as the manufacture of hydrogen bombs and ceramic glaze. The lightest of the solid elements, lithium has been found to have great potential as a psychoactive drug. It is often used to calm the manic phase—the "high" portion of the mood-swinging disorder called manic-depression. Because many researchers believe that depression is at the root of a drinking problem, they have tried the drug on alcoholics. While there have been some successes, the use of lithium in alcoholism is still too new to make it standard treatment. It is also classified as a dangerous drug that must be used only under careful medical supervision.

Vitamins and special diets are also used to treat the nutritional deficiencies that trouble the chronic alcoholic. A few years ago, Dr. Frank S. Butler of Columbus Hospital in New York City reported in the *Journal of the American Geriatrics Society* that alcoholism is a nutritional deficiency disease and the treatment is to correct the deficiency. "For example," he wrote, "the deficiency state of diabetes is controlled with insulin and diet. Diabetes cannot be cured but the control is well accepted. Alcoholism can be controlled with a diet high in protein and rich in vitamins, especially vitamin B. Since the alcoholic cannot be expected to accept a change in diet, he must be fed involuntarily." Dr. Butler suggested that this be done by a method known as precision-dieting by which carefully formulated predigested food is "fed" to the patient via tube inserted directly into the stomach. "A note of pessimism is revealed by many who state there is no cure for alcoholism," Dr. Butler reported. "We do not support hopeless predictions for a patient whose deplorable nutritional state prevents the establishment of resistance. Most authors agree that if an alcoholic will eat high-protein food, such as a steak, every day he will not incur the complications that accompany alcoholism. An alcoholic patient put into a hospital for a week or so and given an adequate diet with intensive vitamin therapy responds rapidly to this treatment. If this form of nutrition could be prolonged, the beneficial effects could also be extended. Moreover, in such a revitalized state, the patient has the initiative to control his insatiable desire for alcohol, at least for a time."

Other specialists believe that there is a relationship between alcoholism and a deficiency of magnesium, an element involved in energy production in virtually every cell of the body. Administering magnesium to alcoholics, some researchers say, helps them recover from delirium tremens that affect many. In still another approach, this one aimed at getting an acutely intoxicated individual back on his or her feet and in command of their faculties in a few hours, the emergency staff at Lynn (Massachusetts) Hospital has used sugar injections to sober them up. Writing in the journal *Emergency Medicine*, Dr. Louis Kunian and his associates noted that an alcoholic treated conventionally may take eight to ten hours before sobering up. One case he reported dealt with a man "with a whopping blood alcohol level" who had passed out in a tavern.

"Ordinarily, you wouldn't expect to get such a patient on his feet for a least 24 hours," Dr. Kunian wrote. "But two hours after intravenous infusion of fructose [a form of sugar] this man was able to respond to questions, although his speech was garbled. We added more fructose and in a couple of hours he climbed over the side rail of the bed, looking for a urinal. An hour later, only five hours after admission, he walked home alert, and coherent. His blood alcohol at that time was well above the sobriety level for normal individuals, that is, non-alcoholics."

The results of clinical studies on thirty patients were so good, the doctors said, that they now use the fructose treatment routinely in the emergency room. In the thirty patients, twenty-nine were alert and ambulatory at the end of two and a half hours. In all, the doctors noticed a striking difference from the recovery of conventionally treated alcoholics. The fructose treated patients appeared brighter and they had no tremors or staggering.

Such methods do not get to the heart of the drinking problem, no more than does a treatment like hypnosis which can effectively remove certain symptoms but not the sickness behind them. Sometimes, though, medication of any sort can help the kind of alcoholic who believes strongly that the problem is a physical one and not mental. Merely by taking a medicine—it could even be something with no active ingredients, what is called a placebo—some individuals might feel they are being helped immensely and will enter a treatment program with the proper attitude. And it is this right outlook that has much to do with the success of any treatment program.

But many times there is a tendency to focus mainly on detoxifying the alcoholic patient, on getting his or her body to rid itself of the harmful poison, getting the person sober. This is, of course, an essential step. But it is the re-habilitation steps that will be important in the long run. Alcoholics are more than just drinkers with cirrhosis or fatty liver. It is easy for a health professional to be turned off by cases like alcoholics who cannot be helped quickly but who require long-term care. It is easy for some treatment programs to cater only to persons with social status and with more than adequate finances, leaving the homeless and the poor to struggling storefront treatment centers or the emergency room of crowded city hospitals. It is easy, too, to send an alcoholic to a state mental hospital "with all the other nuts" and then forget about him. And it is easy for all of us to become fed up with the alcoholic and the "lack of will power" that we sometimes see as the reason for the problem drinking. Therapy for the alcoholic requires a commitment—not only by the alcoholic but by those close to him or her, whether they be health professionals, family members or friends. Some, as in the case of a wife or husband who has suffered long with the pain of an alcoholic spouse, may not be able to cope with it any longer. They are not to be condemned as weaklings or made to feel guilt for walking away from their mate's problem. We are all human, with different levels of how much trauma we can take. What is important is that someone accepts the responsibility for treating alcoholism and caring for the patient as unemotionally as possible.

For those who cannot help directly—physicians who are not motivated enough, or family members too close to the problem to deal with it effectively—it behooves them to find someone who can at least try to work with the alcoholic. If it all does work for the person with a drinking problem, the benefits to that individual are obvious. The benefits to the relatives of an alcoholic should also be obvious. No family with an alcoholic is a truly happy one, for each member can experience the depression that comes with seeing someone close unhappy and in deep trouble.

Lifting the alcoholic's burden lifts your own, too. But alcoholism is not one of those problems that will, like a cold sore, go away after a time.

Eight

The Good Side of Drinking

◆◆◆

NANCY: One of the reasons I don't drink a lot is because my parents would kill me if I got caught. But sometimes I don't even care. Sometimes I think it's worth the risk.

◆◆◆

It is not unusual for many adults to emphasize only the negative aspects of drinking whenever they talk to young people about alcohol. They may do this out of fear, or simply because they are unaware that good can come from drinking small amounts of alcoholic beverages.

The French bacteriologist Louis Pasteur summed up the positive view this way: "Wine," he said, "is the most hygienic and the most healthful of beverages."

Dr. Maurice B. Strauss, who quotes that remark in his collection of *Familiar Medical Quotations*, also lists several proverbs that reflect Pasteur's cheery outlook:

> *German*: "The brewery is the best drugstore."
> *Irish*: "What butter or whiskey will not cure, there is no cure for."
> *Russian*: "Drink a glass of wine after your soup, and you steal a ruble from the doctor."
> *Welsh*: "He who would be healthy, let him drink mead."

In all fairness to Dr. Strauss, it should be added hastily that he quotes numerous critics of drinking along with those who sing its praises. Also, to be consistent with the point I have tried to make throughout this book—I am talking about the benefits that come from *moderate* drinking under the proper circumstances. I am also assuming that it is understood that I don't mean that liquor will cure what ails you; nor that if you're someone who's decided not to drink you should run right out and get someone to pick up a six-pack for you. I also hope that parents are broad-minded enough to understand that education about alcohol means information about the positive side as well as about the hazards.

To begin with, let's make the point that alcohol, notably in the form of wine, is one of the oldest drugs known to medicine. Its effects as an anesthetic, pain-killer and sedative have been known for years. Hippocrates (460– 377, B.C.), the most celebrated Greek physician of antiquity, knew it could be used to fight infection. Ivan Pavlov used it to stimulate appetite, the Persian king Cyrus the Great hauled it along on the march to Babylon to avoid disease caused by impure water. The Jewish physician Maimonides (1135–1204), the "second Moses" who became rabbi of Cairo, knew wine's digestive properties, remarking, "It contains much good and light nourishment. It is rapidly digested and helps to digest other foods. It also removes the superfluities from the pores of the flesh and excretes urine and perspiration. The older a man is, the more beneficial the wine is for him."

Some of the early writers were not so restrained. "Alcohol sloweth age," exulted Theoricus, a sixteenth century German. "It strengtheneth youth, it helpeth digestion, it cutteth phlegme, it cureth the hydropsis, it healeth the strangurie, it pounceth the stone, it expelleth gravel, it keepeth the head from whirling, the teeth from chattering and the throat from rattling; it keepeth the weasen from stiffling, the stomach from wambling and the heart from swelling. It keepeth the hands from shivering, the sinews from shrinking, the veins from crumbling, the bones from aching, the marrow from soaking."

More recently, Dr. Robert C. Stepto of Illinois and Loyola Universities characterized wine as a living, complex liquid. Writing in *Chicago Medicine* a few years ago, he noted: "Among its half-dozen vitamins, vitamin B is most important, occurring in significant amounts, so that wine can be considered a supplementary source. Among the 15 to 20 minerals present in wine is iron, 80 percent of which is in the ferrous form that is readily absorbed in the body. Among the pigments which give wines their characteristically clear colors are anthocyanins, which have demonstrated antibiotic effects, confirming the findings of the ancients."

Wine, the oldest, safest natural tranquilizer, is served in many hospitals and nursing homes throughout the United States to brighten meals and the often drab existence in such institutions. Recently, Dr. Robert Kastenbaum, then director of psychological research at Cushing Hospital in Framingham, Massachusetts, studied the effects of wine on the interpersonal behavior of aged patients. It was found that those who were served a glass of port wine became more socially involved with each other than did those who were served simple grape juice. Friendships were formed, following the ingestion of wine, where indifference and apathy had existed previously. There was a greater sense of security and togetherness. Beer, too, has been shown to improve the behavior of geriatric mental ward patients. In a study of forty patients at Boston State Hospital, researchers compared the effects of administering beer, fruit punch and tranquilizers. Ten of the patients were served twelve ounces of beer a day in a new hospital "pub" equipped with television, a record player and tables with checkered tablecloths. They received no drugs or other therapy during the nine-week experiment which took place for an hour a day, five days a week, in the "pub." A second group of patients was given fruit punch during another period in the "pub." A third received a tranquilizing drug in their punch. A fourth received the tranquilizer in their normal ward setting. Patients "treated" with beer showed the greatest improvement in behavior.

The therapeutic use of wine is not limited to the elderly or the mentally ailing patient. Chilled champagne, according to Dr. Stepto, has been a popular remedy for treating nausea and vomiting, especially during pregnancy. Drs. Chauncey Leake and Milton Silverman, California pharmacologists who have written extensively on the medical aspects of wine, have reported that wine may "provide rapidly available calories for energy production, together with minerals and other factors to aid in tissue repair and regeneration" when used in the hospital recovery room. And a study at the Massachusetts Eye and Ear Infirmary demonstrated that ingestion of dietary alcoholic beverage results in prompt and significant decrease of pressure within the eyeball in persons suffering from glaucoma, an eye disease that may lead to blindness if untreated.

In an address at Vanderbilt University Medical School a few years ago, Dr. Salvatore P. Lucia, professor of medicine and preventive medicine at the University of California School of Medicine, discussed the "joys of wine and its concealed healing powers," observing that the iron in table wines may aid in combating iron-deficiency anemia and in the wine itself the control of obesity. (The tranquilizing effects can lessen the anxiety which often causes a person to overeat.) Wine, Dr. Lucia went on, resembles gastric juice more closely than does any other natural beverage. "In small quantities," he said, "it increases salivation, gently stimulates gastric activity and aids in normal evacuation. Because of its antibacterial action, wine has been recommended in the treatment of intestinal colic, colitis, constipation, diarrhea and various infections of the gastrointestinal tract."

Dry wines (those low in sugar, such as Burgundy, Chablis, Riesling and dry sauterne) are often used in the normal diet of diabetics. Diabetes, the inability of the body to burn up sugars, is caused by the insufficient production of the hormone insulin by the pancreas. Unlike sugar, alcohol is readily metabolized without the aid of insulin and is, therefore, an excellent source of energy for the diabetic. Wines high in sugar, such as kosher and dessert wines, are prohibited for the diabetic. Since every diabetic must be treated individually, a physician's advice with regard to the use of wine or other alcoholic beverage is important.

In a recent issue of *Medical World News,* Dr. Henry Dolger, director of the diabetes clinic at New York's Mount Sinai Medical Center, is quoted as saying:

I don't frown upon alcohol for my patients. In fact, I encourage it for three reasons. Alcohol in moderation lowers blood sugar, it has an excellent circulatory effect in those with cardiovascular disease, and it is also a source of calories, which goes back to the days before insulin in 1918 when the Rockefeller Institute treated diabetic children with one ounce of alcohol every hour. Most of my patients drink socially. Diabetes is not in itself incompatible with drinking.

The use of wine and liquor in the treatment of cardiovascular disease is an old remedy. While such therapy is by no means used exclusive of other medical treatment, it is known that cordials, wine, brandy and distilled liquors can and do control the pain of angina in heart disease. (Angina pectoris, pain in the chest sometimes radiating to the left arm, is caused by a spasm of the heart's coronary artery.)

One physician who has spoken of the benefits of wine for angina sufferers is Dr. William Dock, chief of medical services at the Brooklyn Veterans Administration Hospital. Wine, he told a symposium on wine and health at the University of Chicago recently, is especially good for some patients who have undergone surgery and whose diet is limited to liquids, or who find bland or salt-free diets monotonous. "When patients are at home," he added, "it is possible to start those unfamiliar with wine by prescribing red wine added to water, just as one does with children in a civilized European environment. It does give a pleasant taste, even to chlorinated water, and may make it easier to take a large amount of fluids by mouth." Dr. Dock also advised that patients who want to postpone their next heart attack or stroke have to avoid certain foods, such as salt, egg yolk and animal fats. They should, instead, eat a diet plentiful in fruit, lean meats, fish, unsaturated fats and low-starch vegetables. "Many of these," said Dr. Dock, "are made more tasty with wine."

Some years ago, the Vodka Information Bureau of New York City remarked that despite the advent of modern drugs, physicians still prescribe distilled spirits as a heart medicine. The bureau reviewed the medical literature and quoted a number of heart specialists on the beneficial role of distilled spirits. Among them was the late Dr. Paul Dudley White, the noted Boston cardiologist who once served as consultant to President Eisenhower. An ounce or two of distilled spirits, Dr. White said, may give rapid relief from angina pectoris, usually in the course of a very few minutes. "In small or moderate amounts," the specialist said in his medical textbook, *Heart Disease*, "it has no harmful effect at all but rather a vasodilating [enlarging the blood vessels] action which relieves or prevents angina."

According to the bureau, many doctors prescribe one to two ounces of a distilled liquor, sometimes two or three times a day, for the relief of heart pains, prevention of angina attacks and lessening of the damaging effects of circulatory problems, including hardening of the arteries. (The bureau got in a good word for its own product, adding that in many instances, especially in the case of older patients, vodka is the distilled spirit chosen by the prescribing physician. Actually, there is a valid reason for this. Vodka, a colorless and unaged liquor of neutral spirits usually distilled from a wheat mash, is considered to be the most impurity-free of all alcoholic drinks. If the filtration process used during its manufacture is thorough enough, vodka ends up with the least amount of congeners which can contribute to a variety of toxic reactions in many people.)

Wine may be used to control high blood pressure, and there is some evidence from animal studies to show that it can lower cholesterol levels, too. Researchers feel, however, that it may not be simply the alcohol that exerts such an effect, but possibly some nonalcoholic ingredients in the beverage. For instance, complicated substances called polyphenols, found in plants, and also in red wines, are sometimes capable of lowering artery-hardening cholesterol levels, at least in rats and hamsters. Other studies have suggested that the incidence of coronary disease is lower in European countries where wine is a part of the daily diet than in places where wine is not used as often. One explanation might be that heavier consumption of wines cuts down on the amount of fats, cholesterol and other foodstuffs that are consumed.

But, as happens so often in laboratory research, experiments turn up evidence supporting opposing views. Some studies have shown, for example, that alcohol increases the blood flow through the heart's vessels, while others that it decreases it. Whatever the actual effect, most clinicians agree that alcohol does have some value in the treatment of coronary disease, if only as a tranquilizer to relieve the emotional tension associated with the condition.

Carrying all of this a step further, it has even been suggested that alcohol itself may one day be used to reduce alcoholism. "This is not surprising to epidemiologists," Dr. Silverman once observed. (Epidemiology is the study of the occurrence and prevalence of disease.) "They are aware that typhoid bacilli, for example, can be used to prevent typhoid fever, and that polio virus can be used to prevent polio. In the same way, some researchers suggest that alcoholic beverages—and I stress under certain conditions—can be applied as a kind of psychological or cultural vaccine to prevent alcoholism."

To conclude, care must be taken when using wine or any other alcoholic beverage in treatment programs. Some people, as we saw earlier in the book, are unable to take alcohol in any form without becoming dependent on it. Others simply do not like it. Alcohol should also not be used in people with stomach disorders such as gastritis and ulcers, nor in those with liver disease or kidney infection, or who suffer from epilepsy. In this regard, the advice of one temperance physician of the 1900s makes good sense: "What makes dyspepsia [indigestion] so hard to cure? This very alcohol taking. The best cure is to refuse all alcoholic drinks, at meals and all other times, and drink nothing but water."

Alcohol may produce a violent reaction when it is taken with barbiturates, tranquilizers and other drugs. And, lastly, one should realize that there are no diseases for which wine or liquor is *the* treatment. They cannot cure cancer, nor solve any emotional problems.

In moderate amounts, though, both wine and liquor—with the edge toward the former—do have their place in patient care. Says Dr. Russel V. Lee, clinical professor of medicine, emeritus, at Stanford: "There is no doubt at all that moderate use of wine while eating is the pleasantest and probably the most effective tranquilizer known to medical men." For cancer patients, Dr. Dock has said, wine not only calms their nerves but lessens pain and makes it easier for them to sleep during the tiresome days in the hospital.

Sipped slowly, as it should be, and with meals, wine is, for those who choose it, a pleasant, relaxing experience—far more so, as Dr. Lucia has pointed out, than a hastily swallowed capsule.

Nine

When You Decide Not to Drink

—◆◆◆—

MARION: I don't drink, but I've often wanted to. There really isn't a real purpose for drinking. Maybe when you're depressed, uptight, or to excite your life a little it's all right. A lot of my friends drink. It does not bother me except when I'm at a party and everyone is smashed out of their minds but me and a few others. You can see what effect it has on everyone, and it's scary. I guess one of the main reasons I don't drink is that I can have a good time without. At some parties people even think I'm drunk because I'm acting crazy. Some people feel they have to be drunk to do crazy, stupid things. I do them all the time, only I'm not drunk. I'm always afraid I would get caught. That I would be seen by one of my mother's friends, or my little sister might tattle on me. I figure it really isn't worth the risk, but I would like to try it just once to see what it's like. I'm afraid I could turn out as bad as some of my friends, though.

120

GREG: I used to drink on weekends, and once in a great while on week nights. At parties I liked to get drunk, and I liked the feeling of being irresponsible. But then I quit because my parents trusted me, and I didn't want to misuse their trust. I enjoy the parties just as much now, and I have a clear conscience.

———————◆◆◆———————

Sticking to a decision not to drink is often a most difficult thing for a teenager, as well as for an adult. It can take as much courage to say no as it does to say yes for the first time.

Many have decided, for one reason or another, that liquor has no place in their life, that they can get along perfectly well without it. Maybe they tried it, and they hated the taste, or didn't like feeling out of control after exceeding their limit. Maybe family or religion has influenced their decision, or possibly it's just because they want to be themselves and not someone who likes to follow the herd.

Making the choice not to drink, however, was probably not as hard as staying with it, particularly in those situations where all of their friends are doing it and the pressure is on the one holdout in the room. For instance, you're at a party, and there's plenty of beer, and everyone is urging you to have one. They may just be trying to be polite, or they may be trying to see if they can break you down. What do you do? Do you refuse in a firm voice? Do you make an excuse, laugh, and say, "I'm in training"? Do you take it, make a pretense of drinking, and when no one's looking, pour it into the sink? Or, do you take the drink, sip it slowly, and make it last as long as you can?

What if a first-time date, who is drinking and you're not, offers you one? Do you accept it because you feel you have to to keep his or her interest? Or, do you say you don't drink and politely refuse, hoping that your companion will understand?

There are no firm answers to situations like these, and you may have found other ways to handle them. Whatever you decide, and how you do it, depends entirely on you, and you should feel comfortable with whatever that is.

121

There may be times when you will want to say, "No, thank you," firmly, with no excuses. That can be easy when you don't particularly care for the people around you, or the party is boring. There may be times when you'll want to ease the truth in some way because it might offend someone, or make some people think you're too straight. If there is any rule, it probably is that you shouldn't have to hide the fact that you don't care to drink, or have to explain your reasons. But, since others often don't respect your decision, you find yourself forced to offer explanations, even arguments, to make your point.

I can recall going to a luncheon meeting in a restaurant a few years ago. The person who organized the meeting asked, after we sat down, what we'd like to drink. Everyone ordered except me. I simply said, "Nothing, thanks," without explaining that my own firm, personal decision was not to drink during working hours. Ordinarily, that would have been enough for most hosts. But ours took offense. "Well," he said, indignantly, "I'm having one, and I might even have a couple." He was wrong to be so defensive, because there was nothing in my tone of voice to turn him off. But, nevertheless, he must have seen me as a holier-than-thou individual because of the answer; or, possibly, he felt guilty about his own drinking behavior. About all one can do in similar situations is to let it pass without argument or explanation because both could be taken as preaching by some people.

The best approach to dilemmas like the ones presented here is to talk about the situation with your friends or family, and consider all the options and consequences. You might ask how the action you take will affect you or your friends. And then, which response is more important to you under those particular circumstances. The main thing is to be confident, and that can come only after you've been honest about why you don't want to drink. When you're confident about your decision you won't worry nearly so much about the response of drinkers.

If, on the other hand, you're unsure of your answer, you're going to open the door to people hassling you. You should also remember that it's not rude to refuse a drink. Rudeness comes in when someone tries to force you to drink. A friend told me recently about a young woman at a party who was being hounded unmercifully to drink by someone who had had too much. After receiving several refusals, ranging from polite to angry, the person doing the pestering asked: "But why, for God's sake, it'll loosen you up." The young woman told him the truth straight out: "Because I'm an alcoholic."

There is such a thing, too, as responsible abstinence, just as drinking should be responsible. You should respect the choice of the person who does drink, so long as he or she does it the right way. If you don't accept the drinker in the same way as you expect that person to accept you, if you moralize, ridicule or argue, you'll push him or her into a corner, the only way out of which is to fight back. When they do, you may be the one who will suffer the most embarrassment.

The decision to drink or not is a highly personal one, and no one should tell you to do one or the other when the time is right for you to decide. What they should tell you are the facts about alcohol, both pro and con, so that you can think it out better. You will want to ask yourself why you really feel the way you do about alcohol. Does your decision have anything to do with your parents, close friends or pastor? Eventually, you'll find yourself asking yourself what your real values are, and how much faith you have in them. Remember that at any age it's not wrong to ask such questions as: Why do the people closest to me have the view they do of drinking? Has it helped or harmed them? Has their viewpoint and example helped or harmed me? Do I agree with them? If not, can I present a good case for my side? Try asking someone in your family why they drink, or why they don't. Watch the way they drink, how often and how much. Watch how they respond to others who drink when they themselves don't.

The more answers anyone can come up with, the more comfortable they'll feel in their decision about drinking no matter what it is. Then, no matter what the reason, it'll be a good one.

It's important also that the people who advise others take a look at where they're at, where they come from, why they follow one course or the other. If they're not honest with themselves, they can hardly be honest with anyone else.

Ten

More Dilemmas

------ ◆◆◆ ------

MEL: I drink to make me feel good. Sometimes I'm kind of mixed up and drinking seems to soothe my head. I get nervous easy and it helps me out. Other people are an influence also. If everyone is drinking it's kind of hard not to, and anyway I really don't see anything wrong with it. If you want to, why not?

------ ◆◆◆ ------

There are other drinking situations besides the ones presented in the previous chapter, and most everyone will face them some day. Those I'll ask you to consider now are based on a series of hypothetical circumstances posed by the U. S. Children's Bureau and the National Institute of Mental Health. They are intended to get people to talk about possible ways to react. There is no one answer that everyone will agree on. Some of the possibilities might be right or wrong for everybody, others may be right for one and wrong for another.

1. *A teenager is allowed to drink at home, and therefore assumes he or she can drink anywhere.*

    Does the teenager have the right to make such an assumption? Should the parents set some ground rules? Should the teenager ask them for rules?

2. *You're planning a party and you want to serve beer.*

    Who makes the decision to do that, you or your parents? Is your family supposed to consider the attitudes of your guests' parents? Does your mother or father have the responsibility of getting your guests home if drinks are served? Who is responsible if one of your guests gets involved in an accident on the way home from a party at which drinks are served?

3. *You're a teenage girl, and your date is getting high at a party.*

Do you ignore it? Do you ask him to stop? Do you ask another boy to talk to him?

4. *Or, suppose you don't like drinking, and when your date shows up to take you out he smells of liquor.*

Do you pretend not to notice? Do you ask if he's been drinking? Do you tell him how you feel about drinking? Do you explain that you'd rather not go out with him because he has been drinking?

5. *You're a boy and you feel high when it's time to leave a party and drive your date home.*

Do you call a cab? Do you try to act like you're not high? Do you ask your date to drive, if she hasn't been drinking? Do you leave your car where it is and get a ride home with someone?

6. *Your parents ask where you're going when your destination is a beer party.*

Do you tell them the truth? Do you tell them you'll be at a party but don't mention the beer? Do you make up a story about where you're going?

7. *Your date is drinking much too much at a party.*

Do you hope he or she will sober up before the party ends? Do you tell your date to stop? Do you suggest leaving the party with him or her?

8. *You've never had a drink before and you want to see what it's like.*

Do you ask your parents to let you drink with the family? Do you try it at home when your parents are away? Do you try it at a friend's home?

9. *You drink once in a while, and you see that beer is being served at a party.*

Do you accept the beer anytime, anywhere?

Do you ask yourself whether you really want the drink, and why? Do you consider the particular circumstances of the party?

10. *You're almost finished with a drink and the room is beginning to spin.*

    Do you put it down and refuse another? Do you finish it? Do you finish it and take another?

Eleven

Responsible Drinking

———◆◆◆———

TONY: I can't really see a drink with a meal, like at dinner like my parents do. It seems that mass consumption is more worthwhile. At least you can feel something then.

JOHN: Drinking is mostly done on weekends. You get tired of school and all you think about is Friday and what's going on this weekend. Drinking itself isn't all that great. As a matter of fact, it tastes awful. It's just the excitement of getting drunk and buying it and getting away with it. You have a sense of security when you're with friends and you're all drinking and there's no one around to bother you. There is a bad side to drinking. I know a lot of kids who have gotten in accidents and got wined at parties and made a lot of trouble. I think drinking should be done to get high, so that you don't know what you're doing. I like to drink just so I'm light-headed not so I get sick.

———◆◆◆———

The drinking habits you acquire as a teenager could set the pattern of your drinking throughout the rest of your life, just as your eating habits and your attitudes toward sex may affect your style of living later on. Furthermore, these habits can be related to each other. There are, of course, many exceptions, but there well might be a relationship between consistently wolfing down one's food for no apparent reason, and gulping drinks, or being unable to take the time to enjoy an event or another person's company. Too often, effect is the only aim, and many of us seem driven to eat, drink and be merry without tasting, without seeing. "I hate the taste of liquor," one often hears people say, "that's why I drink vodka in tomato juice."

Many of us, Dr. Chafetz has wisely pointed out, drink liquor as we live our lives—rapidly and under tense circumstances. At the cocktail party and the commuter bar, drinking is done standing up, the liquor gulped with "munchies," and at many a teenage beer party, "haste makes waste" was never truer. The cocktail party, an American event most of you have witnessed and will probably participate in before long, is singled out by Dr. Chafetz as the one he feels contributes much to unhealthy alcohol use and which may offer some clues to preventive measures:

> The cocktail party is supreme in emphasizing man's emotional isolation from man; his isolation from what he does, thinks and feels. People are brought together, many of them unknown to one another, to drink, to talk, to be gay. The drinking is done under circumstances that engender little of the pleasurable responses of relaxation and socialization that alcohol can provide.
>
> The talk of the cocktail party emphasizes this. People do not listen, they do not care. All of us are familiar with the habitué of the cocktail party who, while pouring liquor into himself, pours into our ears the intimate details of his life he would never utter to a close friend. The reason for this is fairly obvious —we do not matter, we probably do not care. It is simpler to share intimate details of one's life with an individual with whom we are not emotionally involved than with those with whom we wish to continue our involvement. Words spoken at cocktail parties are often spoken to oneself rather than to another because excessive drinking creates a pharmacological barrier to emotional and social communication. Some

people even think their heavy alcohol use encourages communication. But drinking that points in the direction of isolation, even in the midst of a crowd of persons, produces a liquor syndrome for perpetuating and intensifying alcohol problems. [Cocktail parties, of course, are not all dehumanizing or events to be avoided. For many, they afford an opportunity to gather in a cheerful atmosphere with new and old friends, and the custom is not harmful in itself.]

Youth is too precious, someone once said, to be wasted on the young. The implication is that young people don't know how to enjoy life properly. I don't believe that's true, though I do feel there is a danger that some of the habits acquired when young prevent many people from truly enjoying life later on. If, for example, some young people's attitudes about sex now are the same as they are toward drinking—indulgence without considering the possible harm their actions may do to themselves or to others—the odds are fairly good that their attitudes as an adult will be equally as mechanical because they will never have learned how to genuinely enjoy. Sexual partners become mere objects to be used when convenient, to disguise a down moment, to supply a buzz—just as liquor does.

There are a number of opinions about the effects of liquor, about the causes of alcoholism and about its treatment. There are those who feel no one should ever drink; there are those who feel it is only an adult pleasure. Some people believe teenagers should learn about drinking from their parents and be allowed to sample liquor at home so that the mystery and temptation to do something forbidden will be removed; others say you should learn it on your own. But out of the often confusing mix of opinions, there is one area of general agreement, and that is that uncontrolled drinking is not to be condoned; it can lead to intoxication, it can lead to alcoholism. You have the freedom to choose whether to drink or not. But freedom, it has been said, is not license to do as one pleases; freedom is "feeling easy in one's harness."

The United States Jaycees, made up of 325,000 young men in more than 6,000 chapters, is another of the organizations that have attempted to create awareness and understanding about alcohol. The Jaycees, like all groups which do not object to moderate drinking, respect an individual's personal, private decision to drink responsibly if he or she chooses; and, just as important, to respect a person's decision not to drink. Most of us, the Jaycees and other organizations point out, *learn* how to drink. As a teenager, you do it through imitation and identification, adopting the responsible or irresponsible, healthy or unhealthy, drinking habits and attitudes of adults. You watch adults closely to see what they do, see how they handle a situation; then you usually pick someone to model your behavior after. Ideally, decisions should be made by the individual, with as little coercion or influence as possible, after he or she has gotten all the facts. But since it doesn't always work that way, about all that can be hoped for is that the model chosen—if he or she drinks—understands the meaning of safe driving and uses alcohol sensibly.

Some of the Jaycees' views on drinking—expressed through the organization's Operation Threshold, a collaborative endeavor with the NIAAA—are well worth quoting at this point:

> Responsible drinking can be honorable, safe, healthy and sensible, and reflects alcohol's use for the enjoyment of life rather than a crutch against it. It involves intention and attitude more than just correct mechanical things. In a deeper sense it may reveal your personal outlook on life. And your outlook on life takes into account your upbringing, value system, life-style, religious feelings, age, maturity, experiences, living skills, and responsibility. In the final analysis, anyone choosing to drink has a responsibility not to destroy himself or society.
>
> Parents or teachers who do not allow realistic and scientifically sound discussion about responsible drinking; hospital administrators, clergymen and legislators who do not believe alcoholism is a treatable illness; business and industry leaders who outrightly fire employees with a drinking problem instead of offering counseling, treatment and rehabilitation; and people who cling to the mistaken notion that alcohol is the sole cause of alcoholism, may all be contributing, inadvertently, or not, to alcohol problems.
>
> An accurate awareness and understanding about responsible drinking, alcohol abuse and alcoholism is needed more than ever before.

Although the responsible drinking theme is only one of many approaches toward reducing the rate of problem drinking, alcohol abuse and alcoholism in the country, it offers the American people for the first time a specific and positive response to the devastating impact of abusive drinking problems in our society.

It can help end the American people's confusion and misconceptions about what are responsible, healthy and safe drinking practices and behavior in our society. It provides a common rallying point for people in the alcohol beverage and alcoholism field. It can add new perspective and realism to the old physiologically and pharmacologically oriented "alcohol education" in our school systems.

The lessons of other peoples and cultures indicate that when drunkenness is not tolerated, when drinking is in moderate amounts with generally understood guidelines about its sensible use, then there seems to be far less incidence of alcohol problems in the population. For the American people, the time to understand and come to grips with responsible drinking for those who choose to drink is long overdue.

Twelve

What about Your Own Drinking Habits?

❖❖❖

JAMIE: My parents are always telling me to behave, but I still drink whenever I want to because it livens things up for me. If I ever got caught, my parents wouldn't talk to me. I know from experience.

The biggest kick I got, though, now that I think of it, was when I bought under age. I was so nervous, but it felt so good doing it. I used to hate beer when I was little, now I love it. You have to acquire a taste for it. I love talking over a couple of drinks and a cigarette. You're more relaxed that way. I also get great urges to dance when I'm buzzed.

Another brief quiz might help you (and your parents) determine what kind of drinker you (or they) really are. Some of the questions were already touched upon in our chapter on use and abuse, but this might be a good time to recap. Be as honest as you can about your answers. According to the NIAAA, which devised the quiz, if you're a social drinker you should have three or fewer "yes" answers. If you have four or more, you may be one of the millions of Americans with a drinking problem—and your age doesn't exclude you.

The test, it should be noted, is not 100 percent foolproof but it will help to highlight the danger signals.

1. Do you often talk about drinking? Or think about it?
2. Do you sometimes gulp your drinks?
3. Do you drink more than you used to?
4. Do you often drink to help you relax?
5. Do you drink when alone?
6. Do you ever forget what happened while you drank?
7. Do you ever hide a bottle of liquor for use later on?
8. Do you need a drink to have fun?
9. Do you ever start drinking without really thinking about it?
10. Do you drink in the morning?

There's a clue, of course, in the questions that indicates how drinking should be done to keep you out of trouble. If one needs a central guideline to drinking, none is more valuable than the advice contained in the *Precepts of Ani*, a book of etiquette written in Egypt about three thousand years ago:

131

Make not yourself helpless in drinking in the beer shop. For will not the words of thy report repeated slip out from thy mouth without thy knowing that thou hast uttered them? Falling down, thy limbs will be broken, and no one will give thee a hand to help thee up. As for thy companions in the swilling of beer, they will get up and say, "Outside with this drunkard."

The point, obviously, is the avoidance of intoxication—advice that has cropped up throughout this book. For without drunkenness, without drinking to excess, there is no alcoholism. Studies have shown time and again that most of those with drinking problems were introduced to alcohol later in life. They started with hard liquor, drank outside the home and got drunk the very first time. On the other hand, the so-called social drinkers usually first tasted alcohol at home, with the family, when they were young, drank occasionally at home, began with wine or beer—and did not get drunk. We've mentioned the drinking habits of Italians as among the most exemplary, and Dr. Milton Silverman, in an article in *Wine Magazine* a few years ago, elaborated on the group's resistance to alcoholism (that seems to disappear in two or three generations after the members become Italian-Americans). "They introduce their children to alcohol relatively early in life," reported Dr. Silverman.

Almost invariably the alcohol is given in very small amounts and in low concentrations—usually a teaspoonful of wine in a glass of water. And almost invariably it is served to the child at the family dining table, within the protection of a strong family group.

The wine is considered to be merely one more food, neither more virtuous nor more sinful than bread or rice or spaghetti.

Since it is viewed as food, it is almost invariably taken with other food, at mealtimes when alcoholic absorption is slow, when liver function is high, and when sensitive tissues are protected by high blood-sugar concentrations.

The child who takes too much to drink is neither punished nor praised. He is not given the idea that excessive drinking is a sign of adulthood or virility.

Adult intoxication is considered neither humorous

nor stylish nor otherwise socially acceptable, but looked upon as a disgrace to the individual himself, to his family and to his social group.

In striking contrast, these attitudes and customs are almost entirely lacking in areas with very high rates of alcoholism—in Sweden, in Finland, in Switzerland, in the United States and especially in northern France.

Protective customs are fine when one is born into them, but many people, obviously, do not come from backgrounds that stress such things as responsible drinking behavior. So, safe drinking has to be learned through education and understanding that there is more to know about alcoholism than alcohol, as well as through example.

The use of liquor is a luxury, and it can be and has been a part of gracious living for centuries. But it can also be dangerous, as we have seen, possibly even more so in young people who have not yet reached maturity, and extreme caution is advised during adolescence.

If you know when to say when, to quit when you're ahead, to know when you've had enough—and if you learn how to sip your drinks, with food, relaxed and comfortable, with friends, and follow some of the other suggestions made throughout this book—then you'll be into responsible drinking. Otherwise it could be like walking into a cholera epidemic without knowing anything about the dangers or the precautions.

Thirteen

Sharing the Blame

◆◆◆

KIM: I believe that the reason I smoke pot and my friends drink, and smoke, is not because we want to be hot shots or to act older. My belief is that everyone hangs through pressure all week, things like teachers, homework, parents and all the other problems that come up. By Friday night, you just need something to clear your mind. You need to be euphoric, and just escape to nowhere. As for alcoholism, I don't think there are any drunks in my school. Drinking is just a part of growing up.

———◆◆◆———

Irresponsible drinking is, of course, a main reason for this country's alcohol problems. But it may be that other factors are to blame, things that go beyond individual behavior. This does not mean that you're off the hook if you've been abusing liquor, if you're someone who can't have a good time unless you're "getting a buzz." No more than telling alcoholics they're sick, that they can't help it, means they're relieved of personal responsibility to seek help, to try to get on the road again.

Still, others can share the blame for the wrong drinking patterns that have created so many problems. Education, for one, has been sorely lacking. Where it existed at all in the past—and often where it exists today—it was geared to prevention of alcoholism through abstinence. The emphasis, always, was on the morality of drinking. Think back on the quiz you took at the beginning of this book. If you were a teenager in 1891, you would have been given a different kind of test, and it would probably have gone something like this:

1. Why is cider a poisonous drink?
2. What is it the nature of alcohol to do to those who drink any liquor containing it?
3. Why is it more dangerous to drink liquors that have a little alcohol in them than to drink milk?
4. What is it the nature of the alcohol in wine to do?
5. Why should you never drink wine?
6. Why is beer poisonous?
7. What has the alcohol in beer the power to do?
8. When beer no longer satisfies the drinker, what kind of drink does he want?
9. Will beer, wine or cider make a boy manly? Will they help him in his study or work or play? [Apparently, girls were no problem back then.]

10. What can you say of any liquor that contains alcohol?

11. Has anyone ever been suddenly killed by drinking alcoholic beverages?

12. What is a Golden Text to remember about alcoholic liquors?

13. Where do we find the water which nature prepares for us to drink?

14. Do we find alcohol prepared for us by nature?

Those questions were contained in a book entitled *Physiology for Little Folks*, written by a physician "in easy lessons for schools." In the chapter preceding the quiz, the author had these things to say about alcoholic beverages:

You must know that the evil nature of these drinks is due to the alcohol which they all contain. Alcohol is a poison. A little poison will injure health, more will destroy life. Children and some grown people have been suddenly killed by drinking liquor that contains alcohol. But more people have been injured and more lives have been shortened by the use of alcohol where it did not kill at once. Alcohol is not found anywhere in nature as we find water in springs and rivers. Now it is the nature of alcohol to make those who drink any liquor containing it want more and more. This is one reason why alcohol makes such liquors as wine, beer or cider dangerous drinks. You can drink milk without fear that it will make you want to drink milk all the time; but no one can tell when he begins to drink alcoholic liquors how soon he may have such a craving for them that it will be hard for him to let them alone . . .

Grapes, as you know, are good for us to eat, and their juice when first pressed out is good for us to drink; but when it has stood for a few hours in warm air, and the ferments have begun to change its sugar to alcohol, it is no longer healthful, but poisonous. You should never drink wine, because there is alcohol in it. Wine has made many drunkards. . . . Alcoholic liquors are really poisons, both to the mind and to the body. They do more harm than war, pestilence and famine. Here is a Golden Text for you to remember all the days of your life: "Never drink a drop of alcoholic liquor."

Today, while most everybody agrees that education is important in the prevention of alcoholism and the promotion of responsible drinking habits for those who choose to drink, there are still many differences about what type of education will be effective. The federal government, through the Department of Health, Education and Welfare, has recently begun to launch a major educational effort, and the NIAAA is encouraging projects in that area.

Another group which has a potential role in bringing about a healthier drinking environment is the one that regulates alcoholic beverages. "Although it is apparent that laws and regulations of alcohol are an expression of how a nation feels about drinking practices of various kinds," says the NIAAA, "only recently has attention been focused on the intricate patchwork quilt of often inconsistent statutes and customs that prevail in the U.S.A." It goes on to point out that if a foreign observer were to view our disjointed and contradictory alcohol control system, "he would probably throw up his hands in dismay at the lack of understandable policies, goals and objectives that the control system is supposed to meet."

Thirty-two states, for example, have alcohol control, but the regulations are a hodge-podge; there does not appear to be any policy coordinated to have any impact on alcohol-related problems and what regulations there are seem to be more concerned with the merchandising of liquor.

Some states have controlled the manufacture, distribution and retail sale of alcoholic beverages by licensing all segments of the industry. Other states have so-called monopoly systems of control which exclude private sector involvement in the distillation of most alcoholic beverages, especially liquor. Two states, Mississippi and Wyoming, run the wholesale part of the industry but issue private licenses to package stores. Some states have provisions for local option elections. These allow the voters to decide what kind if any of sales of liquor will be allowed. Enforcement and tax collection procedures also vary from state to state. Even the legal definition of what constitutes an "alcoholic" or "intoxicating" beverage differs among the states. In some places, for instance, beer containing 3.2 percent alcohol by weight (approximately four percent by volume) is regulated, but is not considered intoxicating. In North Carolina, an alcoholic beverage is one that contains more than 14 percent alcohol by volume. In South Carolina, beer that does not exceed an alcoholic content of 5 percent by weight (approximately 6.25 percent by volume) and wine that contains 21 percent or less alcohol by volume are declared to be both nonalcoholic and nonintoxicating.

Observes the NIAAA:

It is interesting to note that four of the five states that do not issue licenses for the sale of distilled spirits in on-premise establishments permit the on-premise sale of beer or unfortified wine by declaring them to be non-alcoholic and, in some cases, non-intoxicating. The fifth state that does not issue licenses for the on-premise sale of distilled spirits to the general public, Utah, does permit the on-premise sale of beer containing up to 3.2 percent alcohol but defines it as an alcoholic beverage. One the other hand, Utah establishes state package stores on the premise of restaurants for the sale of "miniature" bottles to customers for immediate consumption.

Some states restrict the sale of liquor on Sunday, some leave the matter up to local authorities. Closing hours vary from state to state as do "legal age" restrictions. As of the end of 1973, according to the government report, twenty states had set eighteen as the minimum age for purchase; in five states, it is nineteen; in one it is twenty; and in thirteen it is still twenty-one. Nine permit eighteen-year-olds to buy beer up to 3.2 percent alcohol, and malt beer or wine containing not over 14 percent. In those nine, persons must be twenty-one to buy all alcoholic beverages not specifically permitted for sale to eighteen-year-olds.

One state allows those who have reached nineteen to purchase unfortified wine and beer, but other alcoholic beverages may be sold only to those twenty-one or older. In Maryland, the counties establish the minimum age, generally twenty-one for all alcoholic beverages; a few do permit sales to eighteen-year-olds and a few allow eighteen-year-olds to buy beer and wine, but not liquor. Oklahoma allows women aged eighteen to buy beer containing 3.2 percent alcohol, but men must be at least twenty-one. In a few states, Texas among them, minors of any age can consume alcoholic beverages in on-premise establishments provided the minor is accompanied by an adult parent, guardian or spouse. Other states, such as Utah, forbid minors from consuming as well as buying alcoholic beverages, and Utah prohibits anyone, including parents, from supplying beverage alcohol to a minor except for medicinal purposes.

Bartenders, too, may contribute to alcohol problems. They often serve intoxicated people and are seldom penalized for it. The penalties, when they are imposed, are against the licensee and the offending bartender can go from one job to another without fear of losing employment.

The NIAAA report concludes with this observation:

It should be made clear that the ABC boards (Alcoholic Beverage Control) are not wholly responsible for their isolation from other alcohol-related problems. Generally, little interest has been shown by other agencies including alcohol-control officials in planning, conferences or programs aimed at problems of alcohol misuse. The rationale apparently is that control officials and their organizations have nothing to contribute. The scope of the alcohol problem now being tackled by a multitude of governmental and non-governmental agencies suggests that those agencies that control the distribution system and police the industry should be asked to participate fully in formulating programs to help solve and to help prevent the present problems. Without innovation, most ABC boards will continue to survive, but they will remain isolated and in many ways their activities will be unrelated to the world outside the doors of the bar and package stores.

Maybe you can begin to think about some of these issues now. Talk about them at home or with your friends. Maybe put some of your ideas about how to handle regulation of liquor into a school project. That way, you might help lessen some of the alcohol problems we've been discussing.

Fourteen

Afterthoughts

———◆◆◆———

When I was very young, my mother and father ended their marriage. He was an alcoholic, and I suppose it was she—understandably exhausted by years of broken promises to quit drinking, working to support and educate a son and daughter alone and the depressing effect his explosive behavior was having on the family—who really ended it.

I am certain now, though I was not at all then, that neither wanted it ended. They loved each other once, and probably still did when the marriage was over. But, each had changed too drastically to express it any longer. He by the addiction that gripped him and forced him down, she by being pushed to the limit of her endurance. They had no time left for each other.

My father was a talented fur designer, and he was just beginning to build his professional reputation when he lost control of his drinking. He was in his teens when he got into trouble with liquor, and I don't remember him working much in his thirties, but I do remember the fear that his drunkenness raised in me and my sister, and the embarrassment I felt when he'd show up at my school and either wait outside to see me or, when he'd had a lot more to drink, try to make it to my classroom.

I couldn't love him then, and I used to tell all my new friends—my old ones knew the truth—that he was dead, and I can recall reasoning that, well, he was dead to me.

After the marriage broke up, he'd write letters to my mother, asking to see us, and once in a while, with much reluctance, we'd go to visit him in an apartment somewhere, or in a hospital room, or sometimes in a jail cell. We'd never have a lot to say to each other, and the best

139

part of it was the relief I felt when the meetings were over.

I didn't see him again until years later, when I was in my late teens. His mother had died, and we went to the wake, and he was sitting alone near the coffin, and I remember that he didn't know who I was when he looked over at me. I also remember hearing an old woman whisper, in Italian, as I knelt to say a prayer, "That's the drunkard's son."

Sometime after that, my mother told me that his father was also an alcoholic. The news frightened me, but that was not my mother's aim. I think it was good that she told me also that not everyone who drank had to become an alcoholic, and that my father's drinking behavior had to do with a lot of things that I couldn't understand then. Apart from those things, she said, my father had never learned to drink at home, unusual for an Italian family, but a situation that developed partly out of his mother's stern response to her husband's drinking.

My mother's father, who helped raise me, fortunately never lost his Old World ways. One of these was the wine and the cordials he made, and some of the most delightful memories of my childhood are of his wine cellar in our home in Cambridge, Massachusetts. He made 150 gallons of wine a year, red and white, and I used to get to climb into the barrels to clean them out before he'd pour the freshly-squeezed grapejuice into them. He's also let me sample the new wine through a rubber hose that we'd stick into a barrel, and it was a taste and a smell I'll never forget.

The wine cellar was my grandfather's retreat. It was more than a place to store his wine. There were also barrels of pickled peppers, and salami and cheese hanging from the ceiling. There were comfortable chairs, and a huge table, and his friends would come by on weekends. They'd make huge sandwiches with bread my grandmother baked, and they'd eat them with wine drawn from one of the barrels, and they'd play cards, or smoke and talk. I hung around there a lot those days. There was plenty to eat, and when they offered me a glass of wine, they never made a ritual of it, they just poured it as naturally as they cut a slice of salami and laid it on a slab of bread.

During our regular meals upstairs, the wine was always there. There was liquor, too, but we used that only during holidays and only just before eating. We never had cocktail hours, and I never saw anyone sitting with a highball after dinner. I also never saw anyone drunk in that house, despite the fact that enormous quantities of wine might be consumed in an evening.

It wasn't until I was eighteen and in the navy that I started to drink beer, and not until I was twenty-five and a news reporter that I was exposed to the cocktail circuit.

But I've never gone beyond my limit, and I've asked myself a lot if that's because of what happened to my father and how his life was wasted and because I don't ever want my kids coming to visit me reluctantly. My father died a few years ago on a Boston street, a derelict, not too far from the newspaper where I worked, and I didn't know he was living nearby. If I had, I think I would have visited him, just to tell him I'd grown up enough to understand what he was going through, and to say, "Hey dad, I'm making it all right."

My memory of his drinking has influenced my behavior in a bar or at a cocktail party, just as it's had a positive effect on my attitude toward those who have a drinking problem. But I can't forget that other influence that not only regulates the way I drink but makes me feel warm and laugh a little inside, mostly when I'm standing around in some plush hotel function room, having a drink with people I've just met and often can't get away from fast enough. That's my grandfather's wine cellar.

Answers to Quiz

Beginning on Page 12

———◆◆———

You may wish to retake the quiz before you glance at these to compare your earlier replies with what you've learned after reading.

1. True	15. True	29. False
2. True	16. True	30. False
3. False	17. False	31. False
4. False	18. False	32. True
5. True	19. False	33. True
6. True	20. True	34. False
7. False	21. False	35. True
8. False	22. True	36. True
9. False	23. False	37. False
10. False	24. True	38. True
11. False	25. True	39. True
12. False	26. True	40. True
13. True	27. False	41. True
14. True	28. True	

Glossary of
Alcoholic Beverages

———◆◆◆———

ABSINTHE: A bitter, green, powerful liqueur distilled from the leaves of European wormwood. Illegal in the United States.

ALE: Called English beer, it has a slightly bitter flavor and a higher alcoholic content than beer. Ale is brewed by rapid fermentation (beer more slowly) from malt and hops. *Larousse Gastronomique: The Encyclopedia of Food, Wine and Cookery* adds this note: "It used to be a tradition in wealthy English families at the birth of a son to fill one of several barrels of ale especially brewed for the occasion. The barrels, hermetically sealed, were not opened until the son and heir reached his majority. On this memorable day, which was called 'the coming of age,' and was celebrated with great pomp, all the tenants, friends and servants were invited to a great repast; after the banquet, the famous beer, which had attained the age of twenty-one years, was passed out." (See beer.)

ANISETTE: A licorice-flavored liqueur (cordial), about 60 proof, made from aniseed.

APERITIF: An alcoholic drink, usually wine based (sherry or vermouth), taken before meals as an appetizer.

APPLEJACK: A brandy distilled from cider; also, the central unfrozen portion of a keg of frozen hard cider.

AQUAVIT: A Scandinavian, caraway-seed flavored, clear liquor.

B & B: Liqueur, one part Benedictine, one part cognac.

BEAUJOLAIS: Ruby-red French wine with fruity taste.

BEER: Somewhat bitter, carbonated alcoholic beverage made by the action of yeast on cereals. Malt, which is grain softened by steeping in water, is used to change the starch in the cereal to sugar. Hops, the dried flowers of the hop plant, give the beer its distinctive flavor and aroma. After boiling, filtering and fermentation, the mixture is bottled or canned.

BENEDICTINE: A French liqueur made from a secret herb formula, invented and produced by the Benedictine monks at the Abbey Fecamp.

BITTERS: Aromatic and bitter-tasting ingredient added to mixed drinks. Made by combining various barks, roots, berries and herbs. (One of the most well known is angostura bitters, made in Trinidad from an old secret formula.)

BLOODY MARY: Vodka and spiced tomato juice.

BOCK: A heavy dark beer, usually brewed in the spring.

BOILERMAKER: Whiskey with a beer chaser. (A chaser is usually water taken after hard liquor.)

BORDEAUX: The great wine-producing region of France.

BOURBON: Whiskey distilled from corn mash and aged about four years in new charred oak containers. Named for Bourbon County, Kentucky, where it originated.

BRANDY: An alcoholic liquor distilled from wine or fermented fruit juice. Usually bottled at 80 proof to 84 proof. Used traditionally as an after-dinner drink and in cooking.

BRANDY ALEXANDER: Cocktail made from brandy, cream and crème de cacao.

BULLSHOT: Vodka and beef bouillon.

BURGUNDY: Wine-making region of France where red and white table wines are produced. Burgundy may also refer to similar wines made elsewhere.

CAMPARI: Reddish Italian liqueur.

CANADIAN WHISKEY: Blended whiskey produced only in Canada, noted for its light body.

CHABLIS: A dry white Burgundy table wine, named after a French wine-growing region.

CHAMPAGNE: A carbonated wine, but specifically a white sparkling wine made in the old province of Champagne, France.

CHARTREUSE: Cordial. Yellowish (or green), made from herbs under a secret formula by the Carthusian monks in France.

CHIANTI: A popular dry red Italian table wine.

CLARET: A dry red table wine, specifically from the Bordeaux region of France.

COCKTAIL: Iced alcoholic drink mixed with various ingredients and served in a small glass.

COGNAC: Fine brandy produced only in the Cognac region of France.

COINTREAU: Cordial. Cognac distilled with orange peel.

COLLINS: A tall iced drink mixed with liquor, sugar, lemon or lime, and soda water.

CORDIAL: The same as liqueur. Cordials are sweet and colorful liquors made of fruits, herbs, roots, flowers or juices. Often served after meals with dessert. Many are know by brand names.

CRÈME DE CACAO: Thick, sweet chocolate-flavored cordial, with vanilla added.

CRÈME DE MENTHE: Peppermint-flavored cordial, green or white.

CUBA LIBRE: Tall iced drink made with rum, cola and lime juice.

CURAÇAO: Brandy-based cordial, from the Dutch West Indies, flavored with oranges.

DAIQUIRI: Cocktail made with rum, powdered sugar and lime juice.

DRAMBUIE: Cordial of Scotch whiskey flavored with herbs and honey.

DUBONNET: French aperitif wine, white or red.

FERNET BRANCA: Thick black bitters with quinine added.

FINO: A very pale dry sherry.

FIZZ: Small highball made with liquor, citrus juice and sugar, with soda water added.

FLIP: Eggnog added to a liquor mix, served hot or cold.

FOG-CUTTER: Cocktail made of rum, brandy, gin, orange juice, lemon juice, almond syrup, topped with sherry.

GIBSON: A martini with tiny pickled onion added.

GIMLET: A cocktail made with gin or vodka and sweetened lime juice.

GIN: Colorless spirit distilled from grain and flavored with juniper berries. Proofs range from 80 to 94. (Sloe gin is not gin but a cordial made from the berries of the blackthorn bush. Most gins are dry, that is, not sweet. There are many sweet gin drinks, such as gin buck, gin sling, gin swizzle, but the dry gin martini is probably the best known.)

GIN AND TONIC: Tall drink with gin and quinine water.

GRAND MARNIER: A curaçao made from a secret formula.

GRAPPA: Strong dry Italian brandy made from grape skins left over from wine making.

GRASSHOPPER: Cocktail made with crème de menthe, white crème de cacao and light cream.

GRAVES: A subdivision of the wine-growing region of Bordeaux. (Mèdoc and Sauterne are the other divisions.)

GRENADINE: A flavoring made from pomegranates.

HIGHBALL: An alcoholic beverage, mixed with carbonated drink, such as gingerale.

HOT TODDY: There are variations, but one popular toddy uses butter, sugar, cinnamon, hot water, whiskey.

IRISH COFFEE: Hot black coffee, Irish Whiskey, sugar and whipped cream topping.

IRISH WHISKEY: A blended whiskey distilled in Ireland and containing both barley malt and grain whiskeys. Around 86 proof.

JACK ROSE: Cocktail made with apple brandy, lime juice and grenadine.

KIRSCH: Cordial distilled from wild cherries that grow in eastern France, the Black Forest in Germany, and in Switzerland.

KÜMMEL: Liqueur distilled from grain and flavored with various herbs, including cumin, caraway and anise.

LAGER: Beer brewed by slow fermentation and stored in refrigerated cellars to age.

LIEBFRAUMILCH: A Rhine wine, dry and light.

MADEIRA: Fine fortified wine from the Portuguese island of Madeira, used in cooking and as a dessert wine or as an aperitif.

MALT LIQUOR: Fermented drink such as beer or ale, made with malt.

MANHATTAN: Cocktail made with whiskey and sweet vermouth, served with a cherry.

MARGARITA: Cocktail made with tequila and lemon or lime juice. Often served in a salt-rimmed glass.

Marsala: Italian dessert wine, similar to Madeira and sherry.

Martini: Cocktail made with gin and dry vermouth, served with an olive or lemon twist. May also be made with vodka instead of gin. One of the hard-to-dispel myths is that a martini is deadlier than other cocktails. The truth is that a martini is no stronger than any other cocktail made of liquor with the same alcoholic content. A martini with 80-proof gin is apt to be less potent than a gimlet made with 100-proof vodka.

Mint Julep: Tall drink made with bourbon whiskey, sugar, shaved ice and sprigs of mint.

Moscow Mule: Tall drink made with vodka, lime juice and ginger beer. Usually served in a copper cup.

Negroni: Cocktail made with gin, campari, sweet vermouth and soda water.

Old Fashioned: Cocktail made with ice, whiskey, bitters and sugar, usually decorated with orange slices and cherry.

Orange Blossom: Cocktail made with gin, orange juice and sugar.

Pernod: An anise-flavored cordial from France.

Pink Lady: Cocktail made with gin, cream, egg white and grenadine.

Planter's Punch: Tall rum drink with citrus juice flavoring.

Port: A fortified sweet wine which has been made in Portugal for over five hundred years, and is probably the best-known dessert wine. According to *The Wine Book* by Alexander Dorozynski and Bibiane Bell, it is one of the world's most imitated wines. The Soviet Union produces thousands of gallons of "Portvein" a year and California grape-growers make five to ten times more "Port" than Portugal itself.

Porter: Very dark, strong English beer.

Prairie Oyster: Supposed hangover cure, concocted from raw egg, steak sauce, catsup, hot pepper sauce and vinegar.

Rhine Wine: Light, dry white wine produced in the Rhine Valley, or a wine similar to it produced elsewhere.

RIESLING: Dry white table wine resembling Rhine, or a wine similar to it produced elsewhere.

ROB ROY: Cocktail made with Scotch whiskey, orange bitters and sweet vermouth.

ROSÉ: A light pink table wine made from red grapes whose skins are removed after fermentation has begun.

RUM: Alcoholic liquor distilled from a fermented sugar cane product, as molasses. Some rums are dark, sweet and heavy; others are light and dry. The heavier-bodied rums come from Barbados, New England, Jamaica, Trinidad and Martinique; the light ones from Cuba, Puerto Rico, the Virgin Islands and Haiti. Between 80 and 150 proof.

RYE WHISKEY: Distilled from grain mash composed of more than half rye, a cereal grass.

SANGRIA: Spanish and South American drink, usually a wine mixed with fruit juice.

SAUTERNE: Semisweet, golden-colored table wine.

SAZARAC: A cocktail which originated in New Orleans and was made with absinthe. Now made with Pernod, bourbon and bitters.

SCOTCH: Blended whiskey produced only in Scotland from malted barley and grain, and with a special smoky flavor that comes from drying the malted barley over peat fires. Around 80 proof.

SCREWDRIVER: Orange juice and vodka.

SHERRY: A fortified wine of Spanish origin with a nutty flavor. There are several varieties, including palido, fino, amontillado (of Edgar Allen Poe fame) and aloroso. Amontillado and fino are dry and pale, the others are deeper colored.

SIDECAR: Cocktail made with brandy, lemon juice and orange flavoring.

SOURS: Somewhat tart cocktails made with lemon juice, sugar and any liquor.

STINGER: Cocktail made of brandy and crème de menthe.

STOUT: Heavy bodied and very dark beer made with roasted malt.

TEQUILA: A Mexican liquor distilled from a spiny-leafed plant that is also the source of mescal, a stimulant.

TOKAY: Sweet golden dessert wine made near Tokaj, Hungary.

Tom Collins: Tall drink made with gin, lemon juice, sugar and carbonated water.

Vermouth: Wine flavored with bitter herbs and used as an aperitif or in mixed drinks. Sweet or dry.

Vodka: Clear, highly refined and filtered liquor made in Russia from potato mash, and in the United States from corn and wheat. In the United States it is usually drunk in cocktails or mixed with fruit juice. But in Russia, it is served straight and gulped at one swallow, not a practice recommended in a book on responsible drinking. From 80 proof.

Ward Eight: Cocktail made with whiskey, lemon juice, grenadine and sugar.

Whiskey: Liquor distilled from fermented grain mash, such as corn, barley, rye or wheat, then aged in oaken barrels. From 80 proof.

Zombie: Tall, very strong and elaborately made drink containing rum, flavored brandy and various fruit juices.

Index

151

153

AVON ◆ CONTEMPORARY READING
FOR YOUNG PEOPLE

~~~~~~

- [ ] **Pictures That Storm Inside My Head**
      Richard Peck, ed.   43489 $1.50

- [ ] **Don't Look and It Won't Hurt**
      Richard Peck   45120 $1.50

- [ ] **Dreamland Lake** Richard Peck   30635 $1.25

- [ ] **Through a Brief Darkness**
      Richard Peck   42093 $1.50

- [ ] **Go Ask Alice**   33944 $1.50

- [ ] **A Hero Ain't Nothin' but a Sandwich**
      Alice Childress   33423 $1.50

- [ ] **It's Not What You Expect** Norma Klein 43455 $1.50

- [ ] **Mom, the Wolfman and Me**
      Norma Klein   49502 $1.75

- [ ] **Johnny May** Robbie Branscum   28951 $1.25

- [ ] **Blackbriar** William Sleator   30247 $1.25

- [ ] **Run** William Sleator   45302 $1.50

- [ ] **Soul Brothers and Sister Lou**
      Kristin Hunter   42143 $1.50

- [ ] **A Teacup Full of Roses**
      Sharon Bell Mathis   49759 $1.50

- [ ] **An American Girl** Patricia Dizenzo   41947 $1.50

~~~~~~

**Where better paperbacks are sold or directly from the publisher.
Include 50¢ per copy for postage and handling; allow 4-6 weeks for
delivery.**
Avon Books, Mail Order Dept.
224 West 57th Street, New York, N.Y. 10019

CR 2-80

AVON ⬧ CONTEMPORARY READING FOR YOUNG PEOPLE

☐ Fox Running R. R. Knudson   43760 $1.50

☐ The Cay Theodore Taylor   51037 $1.75

☐ The Owl's Song Janet Campbell Hale   28738 $1.25

☐ The House of Stairs William Sleator   32888 $1.25

☐ Listen for the Fig Tree
    Sharon Bell Mathis   24935 $ .95

☐ Me and Jim Luke Robbie Branscum   24588 $ .95

☐ None of the Above Rosemary Wells   26526 $1.25

☐ Representing Superdoll Richard Peck   47845 $1.75

☐ Some Things Fierce and Fatal
    Joan Kahn, ed.   32771 $1.50

☐ The Sound of Chariots Mollie Hunter   26658 $1.25

☐ Guests in the Promised Land
    Kristin Hunter   27300 $ .95

☐ Taking Sides Norma Klein   41244 $1.50

☐ Sunshine Norma Klein   33936 $1.75

☐ Why Me? The Story of Jennie
    Patricia Dizenzo   41269 $1.50

☐ Forgotten Beasts of Eld
    Patricia McKillip   42523 $1.75

Where better paperbacks are sold or directly from the publisher.
Include 50¢ per copy for postage and handling; allow 4-6 weeks for
delivery.

Avon Books, Mail Order Dept.
224 West 57th Street, New York, N.Y. 10019

CRY 5-80